W0018057

# Southern CULTURES

*Volume 27, No. 2 (Summer 2021): **Built/Unbuilt***

Published by the University of North Carolina Press for the Center for the Study of the American South at the University of North Carolina at Chapel Hill

Guest editor: Burak Erdim

# *Table of Contents*

Illustration by Natalie Nelson.

# Front Porch

Shelton Hedgepeth's pier, Bee Lake, Holmes County, Mississippi, 2006.
All photographs by Tom Rankin.

**I** HAVE ALWAYS BEEN DRAWN to those places that mark the landscape, serve as our monuments of remembrance and guide our way and knowledge of the local, seeming to last in our consciousness even when they have nearly disappeared on a return to their previous unbuilt state. "It's over there where Cedric's house used to be," we might say, giving directions to someone. I am also forever lured into those landscapes where humanmade structures seem to insist on inevitable presence with a kind of naïve arrogance, precariously attempting to coexist with the natural world at the peril of both. Surveying the southern landscape, we find countless examples of the built world that project confident illusions of permanence, environments created for singular and communal purposes that are fully a part of what's truly here, but also what is perpetually going and destined to be gone. This *Built/Unbuilt* special issue, so beautifully guest edited by Burak Erdim, brings insight and conversation to all of this, from the nuances of building a home in a new place to our collective quest to discover paradise in tarnished, overbuilt landscapes.

My first impulse as a young photographer was to make pictures of people, often portraits, with only a passing interest in photographing what I considered the inanimate — the cultural landscape of the built world. I had even less interest in making images of the purely natural world. I thought somehow to express anything visually about the human experience required humans in the picture; to be sure, this was the urge of the novice finding a path with a camera, beginning a long apprenticeship of discerning just how best to interpret, express, and reveal the human condition. I've always remembered Walker Evans's comment to a group of Harvard University students two days before he died: "I am fascinated by man's work and the civilization he's built," he said. "I think that's *the* interesting thing in the world, what man does." Reflecting on my own photographs of what we find in the landscape, of constructed worlds, I discover abiding themes of making and unmaking, the built and unbuilt, the overlooked and the disappearing.[1]

**OVER TWO DECADES AGO,** I met Shelton "Plum" Hedgepeth at a hunting camp in Lodi, Mississippi. Shelton earned his nickname from his work as a plumber, and I knew him for several years before I learned his given name. A number of years ago, my friend Wiley Prewitt and I went to visit and fish with Shelton at his home on Bee Lake near Tchula, Mississippi, in Holmes County. His house was perched on the edge of the oxbow lake so that he could nearly roll out of bed and into a fishing boat. A tenacious outdoorsman, Shelton was driven day-to-day mostly by the challenge of catching that next fish, harvesting yet another deer, finding a way to be fully within the unpredictable wonder of the natural world. With the help of his carpenter nephew and assistant, Shelton imagined and constructed one of the most beautiful and simple docks I've ever seen on a lake, a slender treated-lumber pier that snakes its way through a stand of Mississippi Delta cypress trees. No matter how close we get to the water's edge, there always seems to be the lure and desire of being just a bit closer, to even more fully experience the water.

To build in the water is its own challenge and enterprise, physically trying with the necessary acceptance that anything built there is fundamentally temporal, regardless of the quality of construction. For Shelton, it was all about finding a way to exist alongside and within the wildness of the lake, the cypress trees and mosquitoes, the meeting of land and water. To witness the beginning of a building project such as this pier is a gift. I don't mean the ceremonial ground-breaking with fancy shovels, but the true driving of the first posts into lake mud, the careful measurements in the genesis that determines the square, level, plumb, and true ethic of making, the visual hints that help us see the shape and form of what is to come. Shelton's dock was perfect in scale, placement, execution, and use.

**IN THE GREENWOOD CEMETERY** in Jackson, Mississippi, I look at the monument and marker to James D. Lynch, the first African American secretary of state in Mississippi, elected during Reconstruction in 1869. The way the light falls on the carved relief of his face feels timeless, permanent, like he's been looking across the cemetery from the first morning. "True to the Public Trust," says the monument, just below his face. To look at Lynch is to stare directly at post–Civil War Reconstruction and imagine that time when an African American Methodist minister born in Baltimore could be elected to statewide office in Mississippi. Lynch had become an influential leader in the Republican party as well as in education, was the publisher and editor of the *Jackson Colored Citizen* newspaper, and was a well-respected orator. He died far too young at the age of thirty-four from kidney disease. His marker, funded by the Mississippi state legislature with a $2,500 appropriation, bears witness to that promising moment in Reconstruction of Black political leadership. While the stone survives and still speaks with authority and lasting power, by 1900, the state Democratic legislature voted to have Lynch's remains and monument removed and relocated to the city's Black cemetery. There is no evidence the plan was ever put in place, and his monument remains today, durable among and beside generations of white Jacksonians, some of them his political opponents, contrasting with the landscape beyond the cemetery fence. An enduring symbol of a very slight and fragile moment in our democracy where Black political power flourished, the Lynch monument stands as a solid reminder of history so often revealed through a close read of built and marked landscapes.[2]

**IN 1996,** I drove from Oxford to Alcorn County, Mississippi, to witness the aftermath of yet another African American church arson fire. Mt. Pleasant Missionary Baptist Church, in the small community of Kossuth, was among the many Black churches burned that year. The burning of Black sacred structures in the South and beyond has been all too common. So threatening is the stature, role, work, and social activism of the Black church that the mere symbol of the institution provokes hatred and violence. Fire becomes the antagonist's tool in the attempt to undo the church's efforts, and unbuild and undermine these hallowed community landmarks, a clear attack on the physical structure as well as the faith and thought they foster. Arriving at Mt. Pleasant Church that day, the smoldering fire still filling the air with charred aromas of wood, upholstery, and plastics, I realized that, for all that was destroyed so quickly, the symbols of the sacred structure remained recognizable: the steeple cross, now ribboned with sheriff's tape; the pulpit, rendered a combination of ash and wood but still standing ready; three chairs in a line, the trinity clear, however accidental or intentional no one could know, while remnants of church pews give the most casual observer a sense of the tortured and empty communal sacred

space. This poignant built and unbuilt world of a rural Black church speaks eloquently even in its devastating destruction. Coming to pieces from fire, the many indiscernible remains left by the flames rest beside those parts of the structure so easily recognizable as part of a church, the unseen and unnamed fully present alongside the seen and known.

The lasting sites and structures, markers and monuments across the American South—as well as those that endure in memory—call to us, pointing directly to a cultural history we must understand and attend to. And yet, these same sites, paradoxically, often leave us grasping for a fuller story that requires additional inquiry, discovery, interpretation, and imagination. ⑨

**Tom Rankin** // editor

NOTES

1    Walker Evans, "Walker Evans Reflects on His Life and Work," *New Republic*, November 13, 1976; republished online July 19, 2013, https://newrepublic.com/article/113950/walker-evans-har-vard-address.

2    George Alexander Sewell and Margaret L. Dwight, *Mississippi Black History Makers*, rev. ed. (Jackson: University Press of Mississippi, 1984), 47, 48.

# A Symbolic Project

## Dorton Arena's Incomplete Legacies

*by* Burak Erdim

> Our task is not the simple one of re-building demolished houses and ruined cities. If only the material shell of our society needed repair, our designs might follow familiar patterns. But the fact is our task is a far heavier one; it is that of replacing an outworn civilization.
>
> — Lewis Mumford

**A**MONG THE EXPECTED turkey legs, fireworks, cotton candy, and Ferris wheels, Dorton Arena presents a familiar yet extraordinary sight at the North Carolina State Fairgrounds. Defined by its double hyperbolic arches, the building looks like an alien spaceship and brings to mind similarly shaped structures in sci-fi flicks or at equally iconic contemporary sites, such as the Gateway Arch in St. Louis (1963), the Trans World Airlines (TWA) terminal in New York (1962), or the Sydney Opera House (1959). Predating these structures by almost a decade, the visionary and influential form of Dorton complicates the fairgrounds' seemingly ordinary landscape. Originally established in 1853 with the mission to exhibit and reform agricultural practices in North Carolina, the fairgrounds became the harbinger of the land grant institution North Carolina State College of Agriculture and Mechanic Arts (1887), now North Carolina State University. In order to reignite this mission, Dorton Arena was completed in 1952 to become a showcase of agriculture and technology and to bring together people from all walks of life in the aftermath of the Great Depression and World War II. Now, Dorton's unusual form looks conspicuous and estranged from its context of cow and horse trailers, gun and knife shows, and RVs. It seems intentional yet incomplete; visionary yet adolescent; built and, at the same time, left unbuilt.[1]

This issue of *Southern Cultures* frames its theme, *Built/Unbuilt*, not so much around the transformation of contemporary sites, as it might seem, but around landscapes and modernities left glaringly incomplete. While many of these sites have come to be viewed as parts of ordinary landscapes, the issue's theme allows us to identify and bring attention to how extraordinarily unfinished they remain. The issue includes explorations of nineteenth-century public spectacles celebrating natural resources, science, and technology; the long futures of nuclear waste sites and their inevitable environmental ramifications; and Carrie Mae Weems's powerful photographs of herself confronting spaces of forced production, segregated education, social power, and reform. These accounts reveal that the South's architectural landscapes have always been and continue to be incomplete, representing an abandonment of the initial aims and aspirations of proponents of a progress-oriented New South.

Dorton Arena, with its unusual form and structure, provides an excellent window into the unfamiliar and the incomplete at the North Carolina State Fairgrounds, leaving those who are willing to take a second look with daunting questions. How did it land on the North Carolina State Fairgrounds? Why would anyone design such an extraordinary structure for a livestock exhibition hall owned by the State Department of Agriculture? Was its form simply an extravagant reflection of the Ferris wheels, circus tents, and the ever-popular fireworks displays at the annual state fair, or was there more to this structure than populist pomp and circumstance?

The usual narrative credits the building's namesake, Dr. J. Sibley Dorton, with its vision. A professor of veterinary medicine who became the director of the state fair in 1937 (soon after the fair's move to its current location in west Raleigh in 1927), Dorton called on his colleague Henry L. Kamphoefner, the recently appointed dean of the new School of Design at North Carolina State College, to help him select the right architect to design a visionary arena and modern fairgrounds that would showcase North Carolina's agricultural and industrial products on a year-round basis. In 1939, the New York World's Fair had succeeded in restoring America's faith in industrial production in the aftermath of the Great Depression. Following World War II, state fairs across the country quickly followed suit to light the beacon of modernization, progress, and technology in every citizen and state in the Union.[2]

Fittingly, this symbolic project came at the very beginning of Kamphoefner's twenty-five-year career as the dean of the College of Design—a test for him and the school. Kamphoefner appointed one of his newest lieutenants, Matthew Nowicki, chair of the Department of Architecture, to the project. Nowicki was to work with the longstanding architect of state and federal projects, William H. Deitrick, to lead a design team to develop a new master plan. Among the new faculty that Kamphoefner had brought with him to NC State, Matthew Nowicki and his wife, Stanislava (Sandeka) Nowicki, were arguably among the most controversial figures, given the social and political contexts of the Cold War and the soon-to-come McCarthy investigations. The Nowickis were two of the most prominent designers of their generation in interwar Poland. Their debut in the United States came with Matthew Nowicki's involvement in the design of the Polish Pavilion at the 1939 New York World's Fair. Surviving the war as part of the Polish resistance, the Nowickis returned to the United States in 1945 as cultural attachés. Serving on the international design team of the United Nations, Matthew Nowicki was recognized as the talented young architect of the UN's Assembly Building. This involvement led to the couple's collaboration with Eero Saarinen, by then also a well-recognized young architect, on the design of the Brandeis University campus, which served as a model for a number of postwar campuses around the world. It was in this context that the Nowickis met Lewis Mumford, who connected them with NC State.[3]

Mumford was a sought-after lecturer at the American Institute of Architects events in Washington, DC, and drew Kamphoefner's attention with his thoughts on architecture, planning, and the postwar world order. Mumford assigned an important role to architecture in creating the type of civic spaces that would prevent the reemergence of fascism and would bring together a society otherwise fragmented by industrialization and overspecialization. In his book *Technics and Civilization* (1934), Mumford provided a historical critique of the social consequences of industrial production. At the same time, he embraced the potential of science and technology to create a more cohesive and advanced democracy. As demonstrated in his contributions to Henry Dreyfuss's Democracity exhibition at the New York World's Fair, he believed that electrification and the automobile, along with a national highway system, provided the key components of a healthier and more democratic society.[4]

The South held an important role in the realization of this new social and spatial experiment. Infrastructure and power generation projects carried out by the Tennessee Valley Authority

Democracity, New York World's Fair, ca. 1940. Photograph from the Manuscript and Archives Division, New York Public Library.

and New Deal programs had set the stage for this new model of regional development. The promise of this New South had also drawn Kamphoefner to the region. In order to sow the seeds of these ideas in the minds of future generations, he invited Mumford to provide a series of lectures as a primer to architecture and engineering students. Chancellor John W. Harrelson supported this idea, as it paralleled federal programs to balance technical education with courses in the humanities. To augment these initiatives, Mumford recommended Matthew Nowicki as the founding chair of the Department of Architecture. The Nowickis, who had fought fascism at close range in Poland, shared his ideas on postwar reconstruction. Raleigh, as the center of a new and thriving region, and NC State, as the locus of new technologies, including atomic energy, was a perfect node from which to instill the foundation of a more ethical and sustainable future.[5]

The master plan for the fairgrounds was one of many important projects that the Nowickis took on during their short tenure in North Carolina. Among these were the new NC State Student Union, the Chavis Heights and Halifax Court low-income housing developments, the clubhouse of the Raleigh Country Club, and the master plan for the new capital city, Chandigarh, India. The Nowickis' scheme for the fairgrounds included Dorton Arena, a 9,500-seat livestock exhibition hall; a racetrack for cars and horses with a park in the infield and grandstands with ten thousand

1" = 10'

seats; and a sports stadium for one hundred thousand spectators.[6]

The design's spatial organization and proposed function embodied Mumford's and the Nowickis' emerging ideas on civic centers. It was to be a place that transcended social, racial, and economic divides and celebrated the emotional life and aspirations of a community. Along with other key planning ideologues of the postwar period, Mumford formulated the civic center as a modern monument. Prior to the war, Mumford had proclaimed the death of the monument, declaring that stones erected for the rich and the powerful were for the static civilizations of the past. He believed that "civilization today . . . must follow the example of the nomad." Continuity, he asserted, existed "not in the individual soul, but in the germ plasm and in the social heritage." The civic center was to emerge as a new monument representing the agricultural, material, technological, and labor forces as dynamic components of a diverse, interconnected community.[7]

Nowicki's curvilinear forms for the arena and the racetrack's grandstand were embodiments of the idea of the civic center and sought to introduce the public to possibilities of a technologically advanced and socially cohesive society. The aim of Dorton Arena was to restore people's faith in the power of collaboration between the sciences, technology, and agriculture; this would be the place where the farmer's kids met those of the scientist. Nowicki's drawing of fireworks displays that families could watch from the grandstands of the racetrack conveyed the social function of this new type of monument.

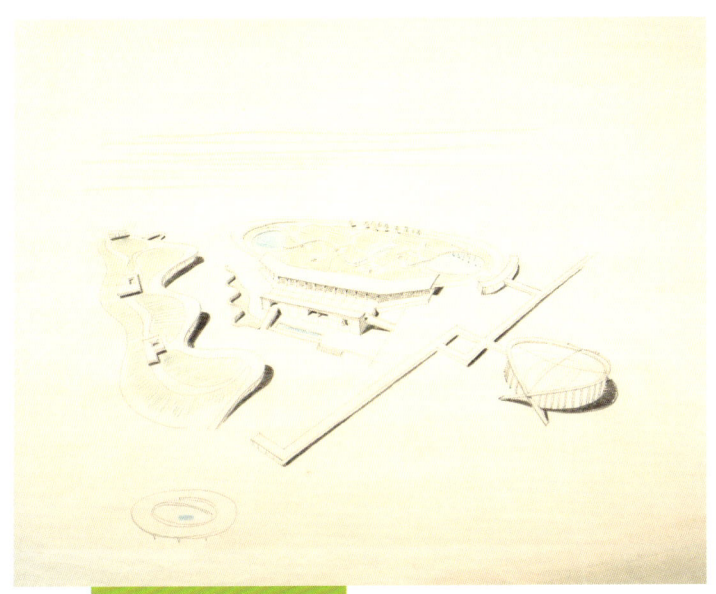

Racetrack and observation building, North Carolina State Fairgrounds, Raleigh. Drawing by Matthew Nowicki, from the Special Collections Research Center, NC State University.

Soon after completing his drawings for the fairgrounds, however, Matthew Nowicki died in a tragic airplane crash on his way back from India, where he was working on the Chandigarh project. Although Dorton Arena would be built based on his drawings, the social and technological ideals that Mumford and the Nowickis had put forward would prove to be too challenging for the wider public. Waldemar Debnam, a radio host at WPTF station in Raleigh, framed Mumford's book as communist discourse. Despite Kamphoefner's continued support, Mumford gave up his vision for Raleigh and returned to his teaching position at the University of Pennsylvania. Stanislava Nowicki, left alone in a male-dominated department, followed Mumford to Penn within a few years. The automobile that Mumford had championed became a key instrument in facilitating suburban sprawl, creating one of the most unsustainable models of land use and development and changing the face of the United States and the world. Kamphoefner, along with other members of his faculty, served a predominantly white community and built their houses near country clubs and white suburbs. The modern schools, built under separate but equal laws during the 1950s and the early 1960s in Raleigh, Charlotte, and various state counties, served as instruments of hypersegregation and real estate development, dividing populations by race, class, and space rather than bringing them together.[8]

The positioning of the new fairgrounds west of downtown Raleigh and near the I-440 beltline can thus be seen as one of the early indicators of Raleigh's suburban expansion and of white

Fireworks, North Carolina State Fairgrounds, Raleigh. Drawing by Matthew Nowicki, from the Special Collections Research Center, NC State University.

flight, which also manifested through the relocation of a number of the state's cultural and educational institutions, such as the North Carolina Museum of Art. Viewed in this sixty-year context, Dorton Arena is out of place and its initial aims unrealized. It stands as a monument to an incomplete modernity and to what we, as a society, didn't build during an opportune time of relative prosperity. Taking our cue from Carrie Mae Weems's photographs, we might confront these sites and reclaim their promise of a cohesive modern society. A closer look at their incompleteness allows us to see them—and, by extension, ourselves—as we are. ◐

---

NOTES

1   Lewis Mumford, *The Social Foundations of Post-war Building* (London: Faber and Faber, 1943), 9.

2   Melton A. McLaurin, *The North Carolina State Fair: The First 150 Years* (Raleigh, NC: North Carolina Office of Archives and History, 2003), 40–41.

3   Catherine W. Bishir et. al., eds., *Architects and Builders in North Carolina: A History of the Practice of Building* (Chapel Hill: University of North Carolina Press, 1990), 350–353; Burak Erdim, *Landed Internationals: Planning Cultures, the Academy, and the Making of the Modern Middle East* (Austin: University of Texas Press, 2020), 153; Tyler Sprague, "Eero Saarinen, Eduardo Catalano and the Influence of Matthew Nowicki: A Challenge to Form and Function," *Nexus Network Journal* 12, no. 2 (May 2010): 249.

4   Mumford, *Social Foundations*; Lewis Mumford, "Social Consequences of Atomic Energy (1953)," in *Interpretations and Forecasts: 1922–1972* (New York: Harcourt Brace Jovanovich, 1979), 307–312. Lewis Mumford, along with other members of the Regional Planning Association of America, wrote the script for the 1939 film *The City*, which accompanied the Democracity exhibition. Ralph Steiner and Willard Van Dyke directed the film, Morris Carnovsky narrated it, and Aaron Copland composed its music.

5   Lewis Mumford, *The South in Architecture: The Dancy Lectures, Alabama College, 1941* (New York: Harcourt, Brace, 1941). Kamphoefner would later chronicle new southern architecture in a book he put together with Edward and Elizabeth Waugh; see Edward Waugh and Elizabeth Waugh, *The South Builds: New Architecture in the Old South* (Chapel Hill: University of North Carolina Press, 1960). Henry L. Kamphoefner, Raleigh, to Lewis Mumford, New York, April 25, 1948, Henry L. Kamphoefner Papers, Special Collections Research Center, North Carolina State University, Raleigh; Lewis Mumford, "The Life, the Teaching and the Architecture of Matthew Nowicki," *Architectural Record*, part 1 (June 1954): 141.

6   Mumford, "The Life, the Teaching and the Architecture," part 3 (August 1954): 172.

7   Lewis Mumford, "The Death of the Monument," in *Circle: An International Survey of Constructive Art*, ed. J. L. Martin, Ben Nicholson, and Naum Gabo (New York: Praeger, 1971), 263–271; Eric Mumford, *The CIAM Discourse on Urbanism, 1928–1960* (Cambridge, MA: MIT Press, 2000), 150.

8   Chancellor J. W. Harrelson, NC State, to W. E. Debnam, WPTF Radio Co., July 11, 1952, Special Collections Research Center, North Carolina State University, Raleigh. Edward "Terry" Waugh, whom Kamphoefner brought with him from the University of Oklahoma to NC State, established the School Design standards for the Department of Public Instruction and designed a number of schools in Raleigh, including Sherwood Bates and Frances Lacy Elementary Schools as well as Daniels Junior High School (now Oberlin Middle School). Hutchins Landfair, "Unequal Spaces: Segregation and School Modernization in Raleigh, North Carolina 1920–1964" (master's thesis, University of Virginia, 2016).

# Reptilian State

## Florida at the American Museum of Natural History One Hundred Years Ago

**I**N THE SUMMER OF 1918, just over a year after the United States entered the First World War, a new exhibit opened at the American Museum of Natural History (AMNH) in New York City. Thousands of visitors to the storied institution bordering Central Park gazed through glass into the cypress swamps of South Florida. Painstakingly built by the museum's leading herpetologists and wax modelers and fifth in a series of museum dioramas that depicted the "home life of reptiles," the Florida Reptile Group represented the largest and boldest example of its type to date. More than twenty feet wide by twelve feet deep, it boasted a remarkable attention to detail in recreating the watery interior of the peninsula. The aim was to illuminate Florida for adults and children alike. "It is hoped," the president of the museum, Henry Fairfield Osborn, explained, "the group will stand as a book plain to read on the reptile life of Florida, as well as a beautiful picture of a part of the Florida cypress swamps."[1]

Scholars who have studied the AMNH's historic animal groups and habitat dioramas—what one calls the museum's "windows on nature"—point to their importance within the institution's educational agenda, particularly in the early twentieth century. As museum scholar Stephen Christopher Quinn writes, at a time when film and wildlife photography were still fledgling technologies, these two- and three-dimensional dioramas "introduced museumgoers to the earliest form of 'virtual reality,'" aided by the museum's claims to the authentic reproduction of flora and fauna. Yet, despite having been a major display for several decades, the Florida Group has been overlooked by historians. Moreover, the diorama coincided (and, in its fixed nature, contrasted) with a period of rapid change in South Florida, which was transformed

*by* Henry Knight Lozano

Florida Reptile group (showing right side), image #36809 from the American Museum of Natural History Library, March 1918. All photographs taken at AMNH in New York City, following museum expedition near Orlando, Florida, by Julius Kirchner.

from a lightly populated, semitropical frontier of the United States, home to the Everglades, the remaining Seminole population, and fledgling coastal towns such as Miami (officially founded in 1896), to a site of massive real estate, tourism, and population booms, including the reclamation of the waterlogged environs that inspired the exhibit.[2]

Visitor perceptions of the display are unfortunately absent from the historical record. We have no comment book to discern public impressions of this miniature Florida rebuilt on the Upper West Side, yet we can glimpse the diorama for ourselves. Photographs survive in the archive, allowing us to contemplate its physical representation and, perhaps more interestingly, the AMNH's *interpretation* of South Florida. Building upon older conceptions of the region as a primeval wetland but, crucially, one now being "conquered" by the inroads of drainage and development, the diorama highlights the fraught significance of reptiles and amphibians to how Florida was popularly imagined, often in deeply ambivalent ways. Such images of a reptilian landscape arguably contributed to the modern US colonization of the region inasmuch as settlers, tourists, and hunters in growing numbers went in search of the crocodilians they

associated with a primitive (yet passing) Floridian frontier. There was, then, an elegiac quality to the AMNH's Florida Reptile Group display. Frozen in space and time, its artificial landscape literally preserved Florida as a reptilian state on the brink of modernity.

## Reptilian State

Reptiles, and in particular crocodilians, had long embodied Florida in the American imagination, inspiring disturbing notions of a humid, reptile-infested wetland that held little appeal for white settlers and the expanding US republic. A century before the AMNH exhibit, when US senators debated the purchase of Florida from Spain in 1819, John Randolph of Virginia purportedly said, "What is Florida? A land of swamps, everglades, filled with frogs, tadpoles, snakes, terrapins, alligators, mosquitoes, gallinippers, and ague and fever! Why, sir, a man would not emigrate to that country, even from purgatory!" Despite his protestations, Florida was annexed—in large part because of American fears and frustration over the territory as a foreign haven for runaway slaves from the South. But Randolph was hardly alone in his doubts about its intrinsic value. While US-born slaveholders established cotton plantations in the Panhandle region, few white settlers migrated to the peninsula, deterred by the likes of Randolph's nightmarish environmental imagery, a hot climate associated with debilitating fevers, and the presence of Seminole tribes that had intermarried with formerly enslaved, fugitive, and self-emancipated Black people and resisted US efforts to remove them to Indian Territory. White fears about race and environment (including reptiles) thus intersected with ideas about Florida as a lawless and savage morass. During the Seminole Wars of the midnineteenth century—brutal, guerilla-style conflicts between the US military and Native Americans—these menacing environmental images cohered with Indigenous resistance to removal (under the leadership, among others, of a man called Alligator) to further create Florida's popular reputation among white Americans as a fearsome, and all too feral, swamp.[3]

After the Civil War, however, American settlers, tourists, and health-seekers began to find an appeal in the apparently primeval landscape. The renowned abolitionist and novelist Harriet Beecher Stowe penned letters on Florida from her orange grove on the St. Johns River. For Stowe, crocodilians helped to symbolize the region's curious lure for affluent Yankees seeking a seasonal escape from the colder industrial North. "Amid this serpent-like and convoluted jungle of scaly root," she wrote, "how natural to find the scaly alligator looking like an animated form of the vegetable world around."[4]

Florida's reptilian nature, however, also attracted elite men who saw in the scaly alligator a hideous beast who was, conveniently, a largely sedentary target; alligator hides became a lucrative commodity and their teeth coveted trophies. "Crowds of Northern men flock to Enterprise [Florida] during the winter, and many of them employ their time in hunting alligators," a Vermont newspaper noted in 1873, describing a gruesome spectacle and ritual that defined the triumph of man over reptile: after killing an alligator, the male tourists — "eminent bankers, ministers, judges, and others" — chained the carcass to the stern of their boat and towed it to the beach in front of the hotel. There, they hired a local African American man to cut off the alligator's head and skin it. The head was then buried for two weeks, after which the "monster's teeth" were more easily secured.[5]

Stowe and others lamented this influx of "sportsmen" whose prime entertainment was to shoot at the reptiles from riverboats, killing them in vast numbers — a cull that paralleled the destruction of bison by railroad tourists and hunters in the Great Plains. For many white Americans in Florida as in the frontier West, however, the decimation of iconic species that they associated with the wildness of those regions and their "primitive" Native peoples appeared an inevitable, if poignant, chapter in the modern "progress" and settlement of intimidating lands. "Like the Bison and North American Indian, the alligator is destined in the near future to become extinct," espoused a writer in the *Florida Dispatch* in the 1880s. "They are vanishing at the approach of the white man's step and civilization, like the morning mist before the rays of the sun."[6]

The AMNH's work, meanwhile, reflected these Gilded Age connections between landscape and species, tourists and hunters, and conceptions of Florida as a reptilian domain undergoing white colonization. In his public lecture series at the museum, Albert Bickmore, founder of the AMNH, delivered talks on myriad places and creatures, helping to foster the public's thirst for natural history and geography. Bickmore's "Mississippi Valley and Southern States" lecture gave insight into what was deemed educational for a northern audience eager to vicariously experience the near West and South. Seventy-two stereopticon images illuminated the huge cinematic screen; states were framed — wall-to-wall — through six or seven visual subjects for consumption, while Bickmore narrated what amounted to a storybook South, exoticized for a predominantly middle-class white audience. For Louisiana, photographs of the Mississippi River and of sugarcane plantations and mills; for South Carolina, Charleston's historic harbor and finest colonial residences; for Georgia, revolutionary war monuments, cotton fields, and Black children outside dilapidated homes.

For Florida (the final stop on this virtual tour), however, the treatment was a little different. Alongside images of Silver Springs, a coconut-lined path in Palm Beach, and an orange grove, the stereopticon displayed slides entitled "A Snowy Egret in Breeding Plumage" and "An Alligator in Okeechobee Lake." Florida, then, was the only southern state to be represented in the AMNH lecture through its fauna, an indication, perhaps, of how much animal life (rather

Florida Reptile Group (showing left side and alligator), image #36810 from the American Museum of Natural History Library, March 1918.

than human history) embodied many northerners' notions of the state. Nevertheless, a link between Florida's fauna and its contemporary development was apparent. The lecture closed with photographs of a lavish new hotel built in St. Augustine by railroad magnate Henry Flagler. "Pictures of palm trees, orange groves, and alligators followed each in rapid succession," one audience member wrote, before closing with "the exterior and interior of the palatial Hotel Ponce de Leon." Named for the Spanish conquistador who searched in vain for the Fountain of Youth, the hotel promised a base of luxury from where health-seekers, adventurous tourists, and prospective settlers ventured southward into subtropical rivers and wilds to where the snowy egret and the American alligator, presumably, remained lords of the wet country.[7]

Their reign in peninsular Florida, however, was coming to an end, according to the message of Bickmore's lecture on reptiles delivered in 1892 to the teachers of New York State. "Wherever civilization takes its place, burning down the jungles and removing the undergrowth," he explained, "we find that these animals slowly disappear." The great screen in the hall depicted an alligator lazing in the St. Johns River: "a view which you may have the pleasure, perhaps, of witnessing, but rarely now, if you should go . . . to the swamps of Florida." More and more, then, this disappearing sight was recreated in distant locales such as New York. By 1916, the *New York Sun* noted how the shooting of alligators in Florida had recently been a "favorite sport" to such an extent that the crocodilian population had become "too scarce for it to be indulged in any more." Instead, hunters were dispatched to capture the reptiles for zoological parks; an accompanying photograph showed two men in a boat in the Everglades, binding an alligator that was destined for the Bronx Zoo.[8]

## Constructing the Florida Reptile Group

A far more elaborate facsimile of Florida's vanishing reptilian wilds, meanwhile, was being built at the American Museum of Natural History. The diorama that opened to the public in 1918 was the product of three years of work in the curatorial reconstruction of Florida's wetlands: first, a museum expedition in 1915 to the cypress swamps near Kissimmee under the leadership of herpetologist Walter Escherich and then the labors of wax modeler Ernest W. Smith, who died in October 1917 before the display was complete. Escherich and his colleagues undertook their fieldwork in swamps and on rivers within a radius of between twenty and sixty-five miles of the small citrus town of Orlando. Many of the collected species were transported to New York alive and then used as models for the construction of mounts and wax casts for the diorama. The collected specimens formed an impressive (and deadly) roll call: toads and Congo eels, skinks, chameleons, painted terrapins, mud turtles, soft-shelled turtles, alligator snapping turtles, diamond-back rattlesnakes, pygmy rattlesnakes, king and coral snakes, and alligators at various stages of growth. The latter species, of which Escherich captured seven from Kissimmee Prairie alone, held a special prominence in their plans. For all its diversity, the museum group, its president wrote in 1916, was designed to "show the Florida alligator in particular."[9]

Opening two years later, the Florida Group at the AMNH proved a reptilian feast for urban eyes. The diorama displayed a reptile- and amphibian-infused landscape to the residents of Gotham. Dozens of snakes curled on slender strips of land—mottled sand at the fringes of the recreated cypress swamp, ever encroached upon and dominated by the water; frogs, poised to leap, dotted the weedy riverbank, while turtles swam beneath a dark glassy surface; lizards in vertical climb held in perpetuity to the cypress trees, from which hung tendrils of Spanish moss and where perched, like a sentinel, a white heron. The elegant bird, like Bickmore's snowy egret, was a recurrent symbol of Florida animal life.

But it was likely the alligators that drew the eye. Way down low, in the exposed crux of a great cypress tree and half-submerged in the swamp, one alligator looked squarely back at the observer. The placement of this crocodilian was logical and scientifically sound. Alligators spend the vast majority of their time in water and frequent shaded patches of foliage in rivers and swamps. At the same time, something more sinister attaches to the creature from its shadowed spot in the far right-hand edge of the diorama. Part of it is the angle. Because the cypress tree is turned slightly to the left, a visitor approaching the scene from the right would not see the alligator at first, particularly given the array of other creatures in the foreground that command attention. Only once the museumgoer had come around to the center of the diorama and looked squarely again at the cypress swamp did the creature appear. Set in an open hole of rotting wood, itself like a gaping maw of teeth, the alligator is hiding, waiting, a patient assassin of Florida's ancient wilds.

The crocodilian menace infusing the Florida diorama played upon the kind of fearmongering long present in popular attitudes toward the American alligator, evident in postcards, travel books, and novels that tended to grossly exaggerate the reptile's threat to and predation of humans. This sense of a monstrous predator was balanced, to a degree, by another crocodilian on display, whose presence reflects the hopes of the herpetologists and curators behind the exhibit to educate, as well as captivate, the public on Florida's reptile species. Eagle-eyed visitors would have spotted, on the left side of the display, well away from the half-hidden, lurking crocodilian, a female alligator guarding her eggs, from which hatched offspring. The AMNH diorama made a telling if implicit effort to link the alligator not with death but with life. But this nod to the persistence of the American alligator was framed within a wider guidebook narrative of a vanishing environment and a species on the verge of annihilation, with the southern state's cypress swamps "rapidly disappearing through the effects of fire, lumbering, and the present movement for the drainage of the Florida swamp lands." See this reptilian world vicariously, in other words, before the real thing was gone forever.[10]

## "Illusion of the Natural"

The AMNH prided itself, above all, on the scientific accuracy of its natural history displays and recreated ecosystems, yet the Florida Reptile Group was, at once, lifelike and unreal. The museum guide hailed the diorama as a "fine exact reproduction of nature." The curating work of wax modeler Smith and his successor, Frederic H. Stoll, was exquisite; so was the background painting by Hobart Nichols that had the cypress swamp on the curved rear wall stretching off into a misted horizon, a true feat to convey within an interior the openness of Florida's wetlands. Animal forms crafted meticulously for the display reflected the mission of museum president Osborn "to bring a vision of the world to those who otherwise can never see it," including, at one stage, twenty-six turtles of nine different species, thirty-three snakes of fifteen species, and twenty-six alligators. Emphasizing the unique educational value of its scientific fieldwork and lifelike wax modeling, the museum prioritized the complexity and authenticity of multiple species together in their natural environment. As Osborn wrote, "The group is not simple; it is very complex and shows many species and many individuals." Thus, the diorama would be "as highly educational as possible in number of forms portrayed, in life histories and habits and in adaptation to the given environment—even though this should mean sacrifice, to some extent, of the aesthetic element, because of decreased simplicity." Visitors to the AMNH were thus promised an unprecedented glimpse into an unadulterated Florida cypress swamp, expertly rebuilt in New York City. "What attention to accuracy and finish has been necessary to gain this illusion of the natural," the museum declared, "even on closest approach."[11]

Yet, in an important sense, the museum's Florida Group diorama was an illusion, a stylized landscape that—like many other images of Florida, dating back to and beyond Randolph's diatribe about a reptile-infested swampland—misrepresented the natural environment it purported to recreate. Elements of stylization, of course, are intrinsic to the diorama as a museum format; Quinn aptly describes the AMNH's habitat displays as "hybrids of art and science." As was also evident in the museum's dinosaur displays in the early twentieth century, the AMNH, historian Lukas Rieppel writes, "sought to satisfy a set of very different, at times conflicting goals: scientific research, public education, and popular entertainment." These goals and tensions manifested in the vision of Osborn, a zoologist, paleontologist, and eugenicist who served as president of the AMNH's board of trustees from 1908 to 1933. Early in his tenure, Osborn stressed how there was "a constant effort to shut out the human artificial element" in the museum's habitat dioramas, but he was also a keen promoter of the potential for these manufactured representations of nature to engage the public and influence how Americans imagined distant, and often disappearing, environments. "Very few people, even among those who have the means to travel, really see Nature in the sense of understanding it, and to the millions within the cities Nature is practically unknown," he wrote in 1911. "So we are interpreters." Osborn thus became a leading advocate of habitat dioramas as a means to popularize—but also to *interpret*—wilderness, species, and natural science through visual display.[12]

While curatorial interpretation became deeply problematic in AMNH displays of Indigenous peoples (categorized as part of Nature, too) that articulated Osborn's eugenicist beliefs, it influenced also the framing of Florida and its cypress swamps as an intimidatingly primeval reptilian wilderness. This interpretation reflected a desire to preserve an environment they believed was soon to be lost, as well as to entertain museum visitors keen to see myriad reptiles and amphibians in a habitat setting. But in their zeal to prioritize an authentic representation of Floridian flora and fauna in the cypress swamps, and given the limits of their tableau, the diorama designers presented an incredibly *crowded* wetland: an approximately 275-square-foot

strip of fabricated wilderness that positively teemed with reptiles and amphibians. Indeed, what stands out from viewing the diorama, as much as the menace of its lurking alligator, is the sheer number of creatures packed into the scene—a cornucopia of scaly life that, perhaps unwittingly, reproduced mythic ideas of Florida's nature as an exotic, reptilian swamp beyond any hope of human colonization.

To their credit, the museum's officials soon seemed to recognize the risk of distortion and the tensions it created in regard to their claims to the diorama being an "exact reproduction of nature." The 1921 exhibition hall guidebook subtly but significantly adjusted the language describing the display. "There are nearly 200 animals in this group," it newly stated, "and *while they would not all be found together at any times*, yet all might be found in such a spot at some time" (emphasis mine). The Florida that museumgoers saw behind the glass, then, was possible only as a kind of still-life compilation: a time-lapse recording of creatures that *might* occupy this single spot, over days and weeks and months. But even this gentle disclaimer was not enough. Two years later, the AMNH's guide writers felt obliged to backtrack a little further, or to make it clearer still that the exhibit was as much a human construct of interior Florida as it was an accurate reproduction: "This does not portray any particular locality, simply the character of

the localities where reptiles are to be found," the 1923 guidebook stated. "Not more than one or two of the species shown here would be found together at any one time and one might pass years in Florida without seeing as many reptiles as are here assembled."[13]

## Reptilian Adaptation

Soon after the exhibit opening, the AMNH carefully redefined the diorama's scientific representation of Florida as reptile-infested swamp. In a museum guide published in 1926, director and habitat group expert Frederic A. Lucas, explained for visitors that by congregating species who were accurately "engaged in the most characteristic and interesting of their varied occupations," the Florida Group was the most striking example of what he termed the museum's "synthetic" exhibits. Their synthetic interpretation was central to the educational aims of the museum. Such dioramas, of which the Florida Group was the largest and most elaborate of its time, drew in the public and helped to establish the AMNH as a leading institution in the promotion of the natural sciences. In the mid-1920s, the exhibit was closed temporarily and moved as part of a major reorganization, with the AMNH's expanded Hall of Reptiles and Amphibians opening in 1927. Featuring new methods of reptile preservation and displays, including a sea snake group and a West Indian tree frog group, the hall also engaged new, important themes, such as reptilian adaptation and species isolation, that spoke to curatorial efforts to share herpetological discoveries and educate the public on the complex world of reptiles. Preexisting habitat dioramas remained leading attractions, including, as one visitor wrote, "a faithful reproduction of a Florida cypress swamp and its inhabitants."[14]

One is left to wonder, then, how many of its millions of visitors in the 1920s absorbed Lucas's nuanced clarification about the Florida diorama—the "synthetic" quality of its reptile-packed vision of nature. What museumgoers saw with their own eyes, after all, was a primeval, reptilian dominion—static, as all dioramas are, and echoing popular notions of *old* Florida—while, down South in the real world and covered breathlessly in the press, there was a *new* Florida, where swathes of the peninsula were being drained to build highways and farms and town lots. Preserved in time and space, the Florida Reptile Group coincided and contrasted with a remarkable pace of development in South Florida, where real estate boosters and settlers in Miami and other towns along the coast and at the edges of the wetlands gambled on fast-rising land values and the marketing promise of a fecund tropical paradise for predominantly white Americans from the North and Midwest. Drainage schemes proliferated as speculators sold new homes and unbuilt suburbs to be carved out of reclaimed swamps and Everglades that had previously been dismissed as uninhabitable—except, that is, by those Seminoles who continued to live there. As a result, a visiting journalist from Kentucky found, in 1922, that "the alligator, formerly one of the distinguishing features of the teeming life of Florida lakes and streams, seems to be doomed to extinction."[15]

Indeed, the conquest of reptiles—and, in particular, crocodilians—formed an essential trope in US development of Florida in the 1920s, which promised to eradicate the kind of "teeming" reptilian domain on display in the halls of the AMNH. "Florida [is] not now a parking place for alligators," Arthur Evans of the *Chicago Tribune* wrote approvingly in 1925, describing a land won, finally, for the American home-seeker. "The newcomer rapidly revises his old ideas, obtained from the school geographies which depicted the peninsula as nothing but a morass, populated by alligators and Seminole Indians, snakes and hairy spiders, overhung with a thick malarial atmosphere." Evans thus reproduced the dehumanizing language long used by whites to describe Indigenous peoples as part of Florida's wildness, while he hailed the modern highways crisscrossing the peninsula, with "great stretches of intensive cultivation" and new towns being founded, even if "vast areas of swamp still remain unconquered." Even skeptics of Florida's land boom engaged the motif of a spatial and temporal battle between human civilizers and savage reptiles, in a state desperate to overcome the specter of its crocodilian past. Satirist Will Rogers penned a humorous take in the *Washington Post* on South Florida promoter-developer Carl Fisher as "the man that took Miami away from the Alligators and turned it over to the Indianians." A cartoon depicted one of these Indiana-born settlers, looking flustered and sweaty as he lugged suitcases through a jungle-like setting beset with flies, toward a real estate sign promising, "Choice Lots – $10,000 Down." Three crocodilians, emerging from water, waited to greet him with giant toothy grins. "Push the alligators out of the way and try to find it," the caption joked of this Roaring '20s Florida version of the American Dream.[16]

Crocodilians, for many of these newcomers, continued to symbolize Florida's hostile but diminishing natural environment. While wax model versions of the alligators, snakes, and other reptiles attracted countless visitors to New York's natural history museum, living crocodilians in the state—often described as a vanishing species, but not yet one deserving of much sympathy, let alone formal protection—served as popular attractions in tourist camps and roadside entertainments. Travel writers likened them to dinosaurs whose existence was doomed amid the rush of development and colonization: "The repulsive reptile known as the alligator," one wrote, "[is] a strange left-over of an era millions of years in the past."[17]

The implication, of course, was that the alligator would go the way of its fellow ancient reptiles, the dinosaurs, and become extinct. In the early twentieth century, both Florida land boosters and AMNH experts had, from very different perspectives, predicted the reptiles' destiny to disappear, as Bickmore noted, "wherever civilization takes its place." Yet, the American alligator proved more resilient to modernity than expected. In late 1925, Florida's real estate bubble burst amid ludicrously inflated prices, and a year later the Great Miami Hurricane struck, leaving in its wake physical and financial ruin. Many of the drainage schemes went bankrupt, too, but left behind deep cuts that transformed the region's water table and the wetland habitats of its species. In subsequent decades, land development and demographic growth in Florida again proceeded apace, yet crocodilians adapted within an altered environment. Alligators in a more populated South Florida took to drainage canals and other human-made waterways, turning up in swimming pools and golf courses, as well as inhabiting their natural, often damaged, wetlands in what became federally protected Everglades and cypress swamps.

As the museum's rebuilt Hall of Reptiles and Amphibians informed its visitors from 1927, reptiles are a complex, adaptable species. Crocodilians, in that sense, have refused to stay boxed within the colonizing visions of Florida as a watery frontier undergoing permanent conquest, its Age of Reptiles giving way inexorably to a civilization of waterside houses, leisure resorts, and sugar farms. Humans adapted their views, too, introducing protections, including, in 1973, the listing of the American alligator as an endangered species, which enabled crocodilian numbers to increase again. A century on from the AMNH's captivating, disturbing glimpse into a crowded swampland of reptiles and amphibians said to be on the verge of anthropogenic annihilation, the environmental reality in Florida is one of fraught interspecies coexistence: however uneasily, humans and crocodilians live cheek by jowl in the modern reptilian state. ◐

NOTES

The author would like to thank the editors of *Southern Cultures*; Gregory Raml and Rebecca Morgan from the AMNH Research Library; and Seth Fein.

1  *Forty-Eighth Annual Report of the Trustees of the American Museum of Natural History, for the Year 1916* (New York: American Museum of Natural History, 1917), 73.

2  Stephen Christopher Quinn, *Windows on Nature: The Great Habitat Dioramas of the American Museum of Natural History* (New York: American Museum of Natural History/Harry N. Abrams, 2006); Henry Knight, *Tropic of Hopes: California, Florida, and the Selling of American Paradise, 1869–1929* (Gainesville: University Press of Florida, 2013), 172–175.

3  Helen Harcourt, *Home Life in Florida* (Louisville, KY: John P. Morton, 1889), 22; Michael Paul Rogin, *Fathers and Children: Andrew Jackson and the Subjugation of the American Indian* (New Brunswick, NJ: Transaction, 1991), 197.

4  "The Alligator," *Chicago Daily Tribune*, May 10, 1873.

5  "Among the Alligators," *Essex County Herald*, May 3, 1873.

6  "The Florida Alligator," *Florida Dispatch*, April 10, 1882.

7  "Through Southern Lands: Prof. Bickmore's Lecture at the Natural History Museum," *New York Times*, March 1, 1896; *A List of the Stereopticon Slides Used by Prof. Albert S. Bickmore, in His Lecture No. 191, to the Teachers of the City and State of New York, upon the Mississippi Valley and the Southern States, at the A M of N H, Central Park, Given under the Auspices of the State Department of Public Instruction, February 29th and March 7th, 1896* (New York: 1896), Albert S. Bickmore Correspondence, box 27, folder 22, "Pamphlets: U.S. Central and Southern States," Research Library Special Collections, American Museum of Natural History (hereafter cited as AMNH Special Collections).

8  *No. 142. Reptiles. Stenographer's Notes of a Lecture by Prof. Albert S. Bickmore, to the Teachers of the City and State of New York, at the American Museum of Natural History, New York, February 13, 1892*, AMNH Special Collections; "Fishing in Florida That Stirs the Angler's Blood," *New York Sun*, March 12, 1916.

9  *Forty-Seventh Annual Report of the Trustees of the American Museum of Natural History, for the Year 1915* (New York: American Museum of Natural History, 1916), 28, 65, 67, 125.

10  *Forty-Ninth Annual Report of the Trustees of the American Museum of Natural History, for the Year 1917* (New York: American Museum of Natural History, 1918), 79.

11  *Forty-Ninth Annual Report*, 77–79. Osborn quoted in Quinn, *Windows on Nature*, 12.

12  Quinn, *Windows on Nature*, 10; Lukas Rieppel, "Bringing Dinosaurs Back to Life: Exhibiting Prehistory at the American Museum of Natural History," *Isis* 103, no. 3 (September 2012): 460–490; Henry Fairfield Osborn, "The Museum of the Future," *American Museum Journal* 11 (November 1911): 223–224.

13  Frederic A. Lucas, ed., *General Guide to the Exhibition Halls of the American Museum of Natural History*, no. 50 (New York: American Museum of Natural History, 1921), 41; Frederic A. Lucas, ed., *General Guide to the Exhibition Halls of the American Museum of Natural History*, no. 52 (New York: American Museum of Natural History, 1923), 41.

14  Frederic A. Lucas, "The Story of Museum Groups," *American Museum of Natural History*, 4th. ed., Guide Leaflet Series, no. 52 (January 1926): 32; "Reptilian Secrets Bared at Museum," *New York Times*, June 15, 1927. From the 1920s through the 1950s, the AMNH "dramatically surpassed other natural history museums of similar size and endowment in the quality and quantity of diorama production." Quinn, *Windows on Nature*, 18.

15  "Florida Enchantments," *Louisville Courier-Journal*, July 17, 1922.

16  Arthur Evans, "Florida Not Now a Parking Place for Alligators," *Chicago Tribune*, November 15, 1925; Will Rogers, "Carl Took Florida from Alligators and Gave It Over to the Indianians," *Washington Post*, October 11, 1925.

17  Florida only introduced legal protections for the alligator in 1943. Mark V. Barrow Jr., "Dragons in Distress: Naturalists as Bioactivists in the Campaign to Save the American Alligator," *Journal of History of Biology* 42 (March 2009): 267–288; Nevin O. Winter, *Florida, the Land of Enchantment* (Boston: Page, 1918), 202.

# Monuments for the Interim
# Twenty-Four Thousand Years

*by* Annie Simpson

> Plantations of the world, lonely places of isolation, unnatural enclosures, that you, nonetheless, are touching.
>
> — Édouard Glissant

I.

The K Reactor at the Savannah River Site (SRS) sits on the eastern bank of the Savannah River, facing west over six miles of woods and swampland, which remain uninhabitable for humans. The reactor is now a tomb for thirteen tons of plutonium, the highly radioactive fuel—and deadliest substance known to us—that powers hydrogen bombs. The plutonium lies inside, encased in steel canisters behind seven-foot-thick concrete walls. The four other reactors on site have been cast in concrete from a void in their own images from the inside out, calling to mind the poetry in Rachel Whiteread's 1993 public sculpture, *House*, a hulking, brutal mass cast from the interior of a Victorian home. The final step in the decommissioning process was to fill these nuclear reactors entirely with cement, transfixing them into impenetrable blocks.[1]

SRS, owned by the US Department of Energy (DOE), spans over three hundred square miles and is considered to be one of the most toxic sites on Earth. Construction on the site, originally named the Savannah River Plant, began in 1950 when the Atomic Energy Commission (now DOE) seized about two hundred thousand acres in South Carolina. The facility is just southeast of Augusta, Georgia, near Aiken, South Carolina. Fifteen hundred families were given just over a year to leave their homes and farms behind, the promise of fair compensation left unfulfilled. Towns like Ellenton, Dunbarton, Meyers Mill, and Leigh were razed. SRS would go on to produce roughly 40 percent of the plutonium used in the world's Cold War weapons. The steel canisters produced to hold the waste are projected to last fifty years. The half-life for Plutonium-239, the isotope of plutonium produced at SRS, is 24,100 years.[2]

For *House*, Whiteread made a complete concrete casting of the insides of a late-nineteenth-century house in East London, after which she removed the exterior: windows, walls, and doors. The house was typical of the neighborhood, an East End family home later dubbed an eyesore, but its inverted details made the familiar shapes uncanny. Window panes jut out at unfamiliar depths and moldings make incisions cutting through the concrete. It commemorated no event and no singular person. Rather, the work is about spaces lived within, maybe as a survival of the Blitz or an embodiment of some stubborn hanging on. Slated for demolition in the early 1990s like the rest of the homes on its block, *House* is a structure's last gulp for air before becoming a memory itself. Alone on the block against grey skies, it feels impossibly desolate, like some sort of frozen specter. All that remains of the work are photographs; the "monstrosity," as it was deemed, was demolished after just eighty days due to public outrage.[3]

(*opposite*) Rachel Whiteread, *House*, 1993. 193 Grove Road, London E3, destroyed 1993. Photograph Sue Omerod, courtesy of the artist and Gagosian. © Rachel Whiteread.

In an ontological sense, everything begins and ends with the void. Pure nothingness, an empty space of potentiality. The void is a zone of unknowing. SRS is unlivable territory, censored from the rest of the landscape through a private security force, gates, and thick groves of pine trees. How much of potentiality is arrested in fallout? What endures in the nuclear hangover?

If *House*, with its un-openable doors and unlivable rooms, imprinted with worn moldings, anonymous evidence of lives lived, was a monument to forgotten pasts and prior loves, maybe it can aesthetically inform how we read SRS's K Reactor, itself sealed, dense, and monumental. The reactor holds the invisible yet still seeping proof of a transnational, multispecies displacement, acutely toxic in a region where dispossession feels endemic: a monument to local ecosystems and landscapes now fused with the American nuclear project. Maybe, though, it is more helpful to read the reactor as a marker, a sign, or a warning of the leftovers of empire and their duration beyond what might be possible to imagine.

The K Reactor is a material node of a largely invisible and intangible nuclear legacy. Waste and the effects of radiation can be difficult to trace due to their delayed effects, immaterial properties, and impacts on less politically powerful communities. Furthermore, the visuality of nuclear sites, much like army bases and prisons, is tightly controlled, giving the common perception that they exist on the periphery, away from publics. However, this is due in part to how American nuclear sites often neighbor marginalized communities.

Nuclear complexes in the American West fit models of internal colonialism sketched by nineteenth-century expansionism. "Nuclear colonialism" is a term now used by Indigenous people who decry the use of their lands as nuclear waste repositories and test sites. During the twentieth century, throughout the West, the US Army colonized local communities in support of war projects and national security.[4]

At SRS and DOE nuclear sites across the US, the traditional logic of national security is inverted, and the threat of foreign weapons is replaced by language around internal territorial colonization and long-term stewardship. Enemies abroad are substituted for the monster we made: nuclear remediation will cost more than the Cold War arsenal itself. Here, we must conceptualize "remediation" not in the traditional sense of reversal, but instead as mere containment.[5]

In the 1950s, for many of the Black residents living on land expropriated to build SRS, which was known to locals as "the bomb plant," discussion of fair compensation meant nothing in the moment. The effects of Jim Crow were compounded; whites owned almost all of the land rented to Black tenant farmers. SRS sits on both Aiken and Barnwell counties in South Carolina. Barnwell County in particular has a median income much lower than the state average, and its proportion of Black residents exceeds the state average by nearly 19 percent. The same can be said for Burke and Screven County, Georgia, which sit directly across the Savannah River from SRS and have historically suffered from the effects of SRS and the nearby Vogtle Nuclear

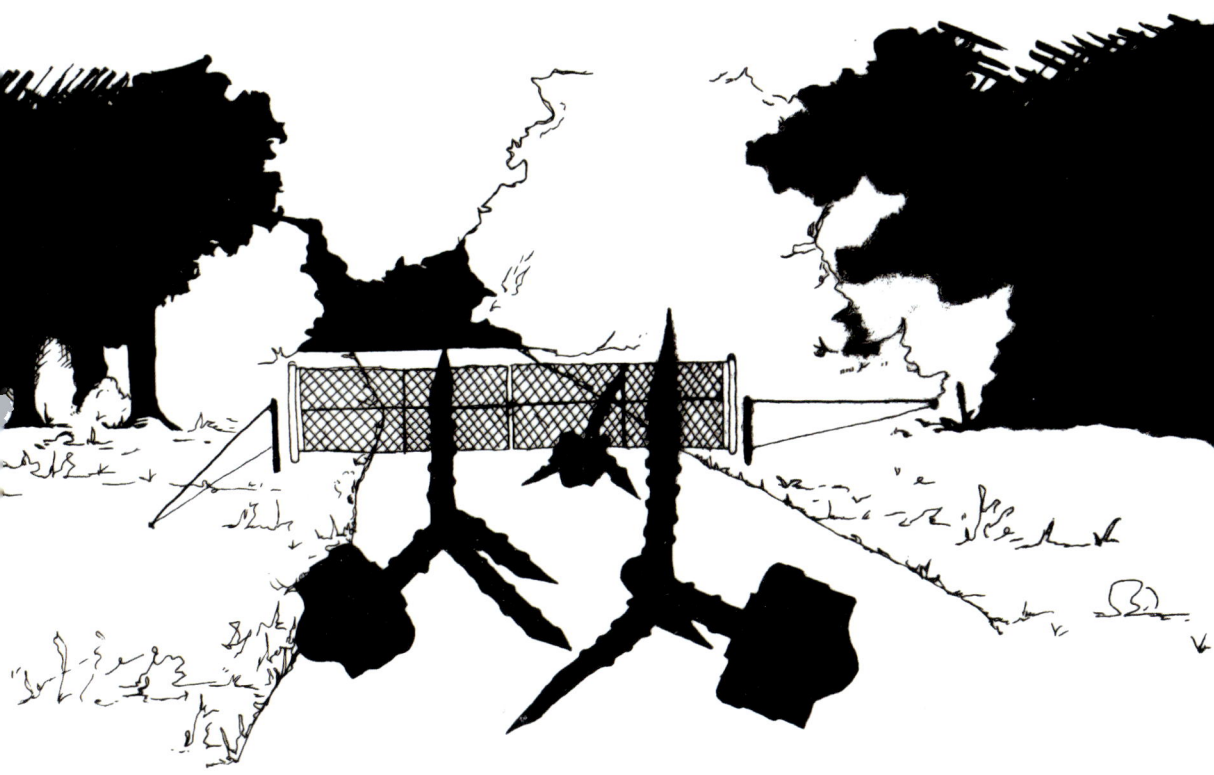

**Caltrops (after Brill)**, 2020. Ink on paper. Drawing by the author.

Power Plant, consequences of a trifecta of the American imperial project, social histories of redlining and environmental racism, and the ruthlessness of capital.[6]

Black nationalist programs in the midtwentieth century already considered the core of the Black Belt South (South Carolina, Georgia, Alabama, Mississippi, and Louisiana) as the base territory of the Black nation, often theoretically situated as an internal colony. Pervasive institutional racism was viewed as a form of colonialism, best exemplified through restrictions on Black people's political and economic power, and the DOE's decision about where to situate SRS rested, in part, on a belief that it would be easy to dislodge Black people from the land. SRS exists as a void and hulking monstrosity, its boundaries drawn and maintained by the DOE as a toxic forever-ward of the state. It pushes lineages of human dispossession forward indefinitely. Furthermore, it is as acutely toxic to the communities around it as it is a problem at the planetary scale. SRS links the racialized (and militarized) displacement and voiding of communities and histories in the American South to global histories of territory acquisition and colonialism. The ground there is deceptively stable, but there can be no full reparation and certainly no return.[7]

Broadly, spatial histories of nuclearization in the American South illustrate that Cold War facilities and military contracts brought far more than jobs to the region. These contracts and installations had the power to remake entire economies. Along with modernization, this new

K-Area at the Savannah River Site. Photograph from the US Department of Energy–Savannah River.

workforce created by the federal government had cultural tastes and political allegiances that changed perceptions of the South. In the case of nearby Aiken, South Carolina, srs brought new residents and new jobs that allowed the town to see itself as a modern, progressive community. The arms race incorporated the industrially stunted region into the modern nation state, playing an important role in the creation of a "New South." As historian Kari Fredrickson writes, "The arrival of the military-industrial complex into underdeveloped Southern communities helped the region to overcome some of its more unsavory attributes. The Cold War made the South less 'Southern.'" Frederickson defines "southernness" by a stunted, colonial economy, one predicated on low-wage extractive industry run by entrenched elites. She describes how future political leaders returned to the region after WWII, convinced that modernizing the postwar southern economy could happen via a large federal bureaucracy. But, modernization-via-militarization was the cynical project of the military industry working hand in hand with southern political leaders to take a hardline anticommunist stance, and in doing so exploit Black communities.[8]

Though the drainage properties of the site's sandy soil and the water quality of the Savannah River played a role in where to locate the plant, its "southern" attributes made it all the more compelling. South Carolina had notably low construction wage rates as a result of the state's antiunion fervor and historically weak labor movement. Atomic Energy Commission officials also noted that those living on the land of the proposed site were Black tenant farmers. Removing them would be easier than at other locations where property values were higher, according to a 1950 report from the Special Committee of the National Security Council to the President. The tenant system in the South was an economic trap for historically vulnerable rural Black residents that the federal government exploited. The complex mechanisms at the highest levels of the national security state include an attentiveness all the way down to how a captive Black population can be exploited in their regional context to expand the arms race.[9]

In comparison, the secret and planned city of Oak Ridge, Tennessee, known for producing enriched uranium and plutonium for the Manhattan Project, was selected for its geographical seclusion, access to electricity through the hydroelectric dams at the Tennessee Valley Authority (TVA), and the abundance of low-wage labor. Landowners were largely subsistence farmers, and the region was known for fighting for the Union during the Civil War. In 1942, the US federal government condemned the farms and gave residents two to three weeks to vacate their homes, crops, and livestock. Similar to residents living on land expropriated to build SRS, they were not paid enough to replace their farms, nor were they provided funds for relocation. The Oak Ridge plant enthusiastically recruited Black workers due to their high unemployment rates. Though the area was not segregated previously, the federal government segregated Oak Ridge and intentionally designed substandard housing for Black workers and residents, often called "built-in slums."[10]

The history of anticommunism, much like the history of SRS, cannot be disentangled from a history of race. The Cold War facilitated and perpetuated the effects of white supremacy on a new foundation, simultaneously in de facto defense of colonialism and in opposition to communism, a movement that was principally opposed to the entire existing system of nation-states. Anticommunist passion during the Cold War integrated the segregationist South into a "historical bloc" in which southern state leaders played a critical role as anticommunist militarists. Southern politicians and industry leaders were by far the most committed and aggressive component of the Cold War anticommunist bloc in the United States. By the early 1970s, the twelve southern states provided the pentagon with 52 percent of its ships, 46 percent of its airframes, 42 percent of its petroleum, and 27 percent of its ammunition, securing a vastly disproportionate amount of government contracts from the rest of the states in the country. For residents and political leaders in South Carolina, a staunchly anticommunist foreign policy made more than just economic sense: it also spoke to their desire for a specific kind of progress, modernity, and a place within the nation.[11]

Theories tying together communism and civil rights were furthered by agencies of the federal government, such as the FBI and the Senate Internal Security Subcommittee. For example, the FBI labeled Martin Luther King Jr. and his allies in the Civil Rights Movement as part of "Left-Wing Pro-Communist Groups" who menaced the social order. The state was an integral component of anticommunist systems in the US, made up of the federal government, southern state leaders, and groups in civil society. These theories also appeared in propaganda published by the Ku Klux Klan in the 1960s; Klan leaders make it clear that they too believed that communism was responsible for the Civil Rights Movement, and added that it would bring "racemixing" to the South. In 1963, a flyer published in Georgia by the United Klans of America showed a photograph of a biracial crowd of children playing in a park under the headline "Are these your children?" Below, it lists "facts" related to recent civil unrest predicated by "the Communist Party" and "Martin Luther King's organization." In this context, SRS, and in particular the K Reactor, can be read within a regional history of twentieth-century white supremacist monuments that sought to enforce a racist social order through intimidation and denigration.[12]

## II.

The field of nuclear semiotics arose in 1981 when the DOE and Bechtel Corp convened the Human Interference Taskforce, a team including nuclear physicists, anthropologists, and behavioral scientists. They were tasked with designing warning signs and markers to deter human intrusion into Yucca Mountain, a proposed deep geological nuclear waste repository in Nevada. To store highly radioactive nuclear waste, we must both contain it and maintain that it will not be disturbed for ten thousand to twenty thousand years.[13]

In 1996, the DOE, this time with Sandia National Laboratories, managed by a Lockheed Martin subsidiary, again convened a group of scientists, anthropologists, and artists to design markers for the Waste Isolation Pilot Plant, another proposed deep geological nuclear waste repository, outside of Carlsbad, New Mexico. In one subsection of the report, "Expert Judgment on Markers to Deter Inadvertent Human Intrusion into the Waste Isolation Pilot Plant," environmental designer Michael Brill and others on the panel came up with marker proposals with titles like "Forbidding Blocks" and "Landscape of Thorns," constructed of "shapes meant to hurt the body and communicate danger" from materials like basalt and granite. These markers, meant to warn against unintentional human interference, took the form of monumental landscapes, colossal forms dominating vast swaths of land. The reasoning was that even if you were unable to communicate a discrete message, a landscape's menacing disposition, marked by looming spikes or rubble, would be unsettling enough to dissuade those who stumbled upon it.[14]

Though some Roman concrete has endured from around 150 BCE to today, the K Reactor likely will not outlast the half-life of the plutonium it contains, long enough for its unsettling form to caution those who might encounter it. The expected lifespan for industrial concrete in underground nuclear waste repositories is five hundred years if the concrete does not freeze or thaw or come into contact with leaching water, just two of many possible variables which would shorten the concrete's lifespan. The Savannah River Site itself is a massive en-

Diagram/location of SRS. Black projection added by the author. Photographs from NASA (Blue Marble).

vironmental problem; classified by the EPA as a Superfund site, it stores thirty-four million gallons of high-level radioactive waste. Yet, it exists within a uniquely modern contradiction: despite the toxic and deadly nuclear hangover (a symptom of a markedly American forever-war machine) that yawns open in front of us, echoing into the next however many thousands of years, SRS has been publicized by the nuclear state as an ecological reserve preserved in time.[15]

I went on one of the few tours offered every year at SRS. Entering SRS feels a bit like driving onto an army base. To take a tour, you must be a US citizen and provide two forms of proper identification at the badge office, before your reserved time. The Department of Energy contracts a management company, Savannah River Nuclear Solutions, to maintain SRS and a private paramilitary for security services. During the bus ride through the site, our guide talked about the site's biodiversity, responsible pine logging, and the safety brought by annual deer hunts "intended to lower the incidence of animal-vehicle collisions on the site." (Similarly, media attention paid to the Chernobyl zone suggests that the territory has returned to a state of natural order: tour agencies promote the zone as a preserve teeming with wildlife.) Woodsy, almost kitschy, Smokey the Bear-esque signs remind drivers of the dangers of wildfires. Other signs encourage motorists to fasten their seatbelts to "further their lives." These are not the warning signs I expected to see here. It's all by design that you could traverse the site six ways to Sunday and not see one trefoil. Aside from the guards and checkpoints, it's all so palatable, excruciatingly ordinary.[16]

View from bus tour, 2020. Photograph by James Enos.

On this tour, I was given a small firstaid kit and a bottle of hand sanitizer (which, granted, means something different now than when I first toured the site in February 2020). If it's raining, the guide might remind you that the bus stairs are slippery. There is a lot of talk of safety here, where 40 percent of the world's Cold War plutonium was produced, but mainly the type of safety that prevents slip and falls, or at least releases SRS from liability if you eat it on the steps. These public relations moves to rebrand the site stand in stark contrast to how former SRS employees remember safety. Across demographics, they recall the pressures to keep silent about their exposure, the difficulty in obtaining exposure records, and how company surveillance led them to understand their employer as deceitful. Plant officials insisted the facility was safe, attempting to dismiss concerns even as evidence of death and illness from hazardous materials grew. Contaminated waste was dumped into unmarked pits with no safeguards to prevent it from seeping into groundwater.[17]

Everyone was downwind, but not everyone was downwind equally. Studies show us that female workers were less likely than males to be monitored for occupational radiation exposure, and they were also more likely to have incomplete dose histories that would hinder compensation for illnesses related to these exposures. Black workers were more likely than non-Black workers to have a detectable radiation dose and to experience higher incidents of some cancers as well as early deaths.[18]

In the mid-1980s, when DuPont still operated SRS, critics questioned the adequacy of monitoring and safety standards. In response, DuPont promoted, rather than tested, the efficacy of their current practices. This comes as no surprise. Their focus on confirming workplace safety for the sake of public relations, not worker health and well-being, fits a pattern. Nuclear work demands secrecy and a closing of ranks as it tangles with discourses of duty and patriotism.

The US military met civilian protests of destruction at military sites across the country in the 1960s and 1970s with claims that their properties inadvertently created animal sanctuaries endangered by civilian land practices: conservation by serendipity. Abundant wildlife shows up again and again in militarized environments; war zones and buffer zones between warring states seem to suggest that sometimes human conflict is a blessing for nonhumans. Certain Cold War frontiers (such as the DMZ) surprisingly became nature reserves, but, by the early 1990s, 81 percent of US federal facilities on the National Priorities List for waste cleanup belonged to the military. Moreover, at the end of the Cold War, the US military faced a crisis of legitimacy: how could it justify continued occupation of millions of acres of national land? Here, military environmentalism serves as a way to legitimate control over the territory. These transformations are not so much a way of turning the US military "green" but, rather, a way to repackage the war arm of the US in eco-friendly wrapping. For example, functionally obsolete US military bases can be converted to reserves in accordance with the Base Realignment and Closure process, which began in 1988. This allows the DOD to spend less on decontaminating the most heavily polluted lands, ultimately undermining potential benefits to wildlife. NATO facilitated a transnational network of military environmentalism post–Cold War, including environmental policy statements that encouraged soldiers to "train green." Though NATO signatories, including the US, have begun to introduce recycling, reduce carbon emissions, and develop "green weaponry," the life-enhancing aspirations of sustainability initiatives and the deadly objectives that serve as the foundation for military purposes are fundamentally at odds.[19]

This being said, a reading of military environmentalism at SRS would be incomplete without understanding how nonhuman life exists at the site, perhaps in opposition to human and military territorial control. Upper Three Runs Creek, which originates near Aiken, South Carolina, runs nearly two thirds of its length through SRS before joining the Savannah River. It is the most species-rich stream in North America, and the second-most in the world. Studies from the 1970s and the 2010s have shown that thirty-plus years of continued use by the Department of Energy has not had a detrimental impact on the creek. There is no data to compare the state of Upper Three Runs Creek before it was seized by the Atomic Energy Commission, when it would have been surrounded by farmland. According to the National priorities List Site Narrative for SRS, which established SRS as an EPA Superfund site, a small quantity of depleted uranium was released in January 1984 into Upper Three Runs Creek.[20]

## III.

I wasn't expecting the SRS bus tour to remind me of tours I've taken of plantations and historic houses in the South. In fact, the SRS tour fits neatly alongside other manifestations of heritage tourism in the region. These tours reveal how we negotiate past and present, and far too often, there is celebration of moonlight and magnolias and the containment (if not outright denial) of the site's horrors. The South is continually deployed for profit, whether for haunting or reveling. But unlike the imaginary "Old South" presented on plantation tours, the primary narrative at SRS advances the "New South" of modernization and economic development. Noticeably, at SRS and these former plantations, the landscapes have been ideologically (if not also anthropomorphically) reconstructed from sites of labor, extracted by violence and coercion, to sites of leisure. They allow visitors to participate in a comforting narrative that makes sense of a cruel history, one that implicates them, without having to come to terms with the material reality that sustains it. History is resolved, buried and done with, but the relics are dusted and tidy and neatly arranged for our viewing pleasure.

Yet, a future nuclear apocalypse is not some wavering vision just beyond the horizon, deterred by weapons or deferred by politics. It is not a fear that haunted those in the past, relegated to the history books at the end of the Cold War. Rather, it is one we have inhabited since July 1945. After the first successful detonation of a plutonium bomb at the Trinity test site in New Mexico, we entered a postnuclear environment *of our own making*. The militarization and nuclearization of three hundred–plus square miles of swamps, Spanish moss, cicadas, and steel occupied by SRS not only triggered a process of re-wilding, but now must be maintained, for there is no fixing this nuclear problem. We will have to stay on nodding terms with it for more than twenty thousand years.

For me, living in the South means to often fall in and out of time, for our history here is not just deeply formative but impossibly present. Just as I reside within the region's heavy history, it also resides within me—that whole thing about gazing into the abyss and it gazing back. If my own past is bound so inextricably to the history of this place, how do I reconcile that with how white people in the South so often recall and represent the past inaccurately? It is true, despite geography, in the words of theorist Andreas Huyssen, that remembering is always entangled with forgetting, and our memories are "always transitory, notoriously unreliable, and haunted by forgetting," but there is something sinister in the way we white southerners

**Fence (after Brill)**, 2020. Ink on paper. Drawing by the author.

fail to recollect what actually happened here, who planted all these fabled magnolias. Nostalgic white southerners invested in ahistorical visions of the region's past seem to be longing for both return and absolution, but not a true reckoning, as BIPOC southerners have long advocated. The "New South" that trickled out of SRS brought modernization, but for whom, and why, and at what cost? Faulknerian visions where property rights and resource extraction undergird race and violence, the anachronistic architecture of our universities, plantations turned right into prisons or military bases—all reach back with a threatening nostalgia for an antebellum South that did not endure in reality as long as it has in corrupted imagination.[21]

The fate of the South, from colonial settlement to the transatlantic slave trade to the Cold War and SRS, is inescapably bound up with an international geopolitical context through material and durational entanglements. How can our relationship with time—slippery, and bobbing up and down in waves of what was and wasn't—contend with a scale as massive as twenty thousand years? All I know for sure is that it exists outside of a humanist approach to time itself. Different from what we were taught to imagine—a spectacular, and cinematic, mutually assured destruction—the nuclear apocalypse plays out daily in background radiation, bodies, biospheres, watersheds, wildlife, and sacrifice. Yet, this new kind of nature, one marked by the dispersal of nuclear materials into the environment, is wild and mutant, diffuse and discrete; radioactive tumbleweeds and toxic alligators weave beyond state control, past the fences, gates, signs at not just SRS, but Los Alamos, and Trinity, and Hanford, and Carlsbad, and Oak Ridge, and Yucca Mountain, and, and, and.

IT-IS-HARD-TO
UNDERSTANDWHY
OUR-TOWN-MUST
BE-DESTROYED-TO
MAKE-A-BOMB-THAT
WILL-DESTROY-SomE onE
ELSES-TOWN-THAT-THEY
LOVE-AS-MUCH-AS-WE-LOVE
OURS — BUT-WE-FEEL-THAT
THEY-PICKED-NOT-ONE-JUST
THE-BEST-SPOT-IN-THE-US
BUT-IN-THE-WORLD

ELLENTON
INCORPORATED

WE LOVE THESE
DEAR HEARTS
AND GENTLE PEOPLE
WHO LIVE
IN OUR
HOME TOWN

## IV.

The warning signs to keep trespassers out deflect from the reality that these sites might trespass on us, that they cannot keep all of the effects of the site *in*, despite public rhetoric of containment and security. This rhetoric leans heavily on commemoration of patriotism and language of honor and duty to communicate not only authority but deference to a greater good.

To understand SRS as a commemorative landscape as well as a proposed ecological reserve and militarized landscape, we must approach it as distinct from geological topography: landscape is a process. Constructed spaces represent and enact popular ideas about our imagined pasts and futures. Specifically, we can look to historic South Carolina roadside markers memorializing and historicizing SRS. We can investigate how what these markers say (narrate a particular story about the land) distracts us from what they do (use that narrative to advance a particular political and social agenda). These roadside markers retell history through their structural properties and textual refrences. Yet, they are able to convey the appearance of an official history through their relative lack of ornamentation, compared to most monuments and memorials. In the case of these markers, ideology attaches a normative component to aesthetics, meaning that the markers adopt an unmediated voice. This voice uses facts from one possible version of history to cast subjective preferences as objective and legitimate. On the other hand, monuments of conquerors make their agenda clear through sculpted bodies towering over publics, declarative epigraphs, and positions in high-traffic public spaces. The unadorned, state-sponsored aesthetic of peripheral highway historical markers, and their ubiquity, enhances their rhetorical power, marking these as official narratives and perhaps flattening historical and political complexities.[22]

The four South Carolina historic markers located at SRS commemorate the reactor with the best safety record (P Reactor marker); the largest reactor with six hundred positions for fuel rods and control rods (R Reactor marker); the first detection of a neutrino, a subatomic particle (Savannah River Plant marker); and the location of the former Ellenton post office (site of Ellenton marker). Two of these four markers, the P Reactor marker and the R Reactor marker, were erected in 2008 and sponsored by the US Department of Energy, with the expressed intent of "commemorating the role both reactors played towards winning the Cold War." The language used on both is exemplary, focusing only on the highlights of each reactor. These two markers are located on roads only accessible to employees and officials with issued credentials.[23]

At the stoplight just a few tenths of a mile north of one of SRS's main credentialed entry points, the Savannah River Plant marker sits among a constellation of RV park advertisements, a speed limit sign, a ground-level DOE billboard, and a sign marking the boundary of US government property. The ground underneath the marker, erected in 2004 by the Aiken County Historical Society, was once paved, but it's mainly crabgrass and litter now. The text lays out the plant's significant role in national defense during the Cold War, then relays scientific anecdotes relating to the site after mentioning how its creation required "moving all residents from their homes."[24]

The last reactor at SRS was shut down in 1992, and the Cold War Preservation Program at SRS began in 1997. The National Historic Preservation Act of 1966 is a federal law that requires all federal agencies to consider the impacts to historic properties in all their undertakings. The Cold War Preservation Program in part works to ensure compliance with NHPA; part of this process required that they survey 732 facilities in 2002.[25]

A granite plinth dedicated to "the families who originally lived on this property and to the patriotic men and women who have made possible the safe operations and successful missions" of the project lies in an overgrown garden off of Atomic Road, which bisects the western part of SRS. The benches near that plinth, which was erected in 2000 to commemorate fifty years of SRS, are so thickly covered with lichen that it's difficult to imagine anyone sitting on them. By the road, a few yards from the monument, stands the Site of Ellenton marker (erected in 1993 by the Ellenton Reunion Organization). The marker, at the former location of Ellenton's ca. 1873 post office, describes how the town was chartered in 1880. It simply states how the town and surrounding area were "purchased by US Govt in early 1950s for establishment of Savannah River Plant." Every year since 1972, displaced families from Ellenton have gathered on the second Sunday in June to remember the town they lost.[26]

Atomic Road itself is dotted with signs telling motorists that they are not permitted to pull over, stop, or get out of their car. At the monument viewing area, there are two parking spots and a large sign that prohibits picnicking and camping. Per signage, parking is only allowed for those viewing the marker.

SRS markers illustrate a fictional history of linear progress and success, though all four were erected between 1992 and 2008: nearly nominal sacrifice for the greater good. Forced dispossession, in its many forms across species on irradiated soil (which has seen slavery and genocide, too) becomes interchangeable with patriotism. For SRS employees, staying quiet about radiation exposure and the DOE's illegal dumping is framed as a duty. Those who speak out risk that their employer will surveil them and their families.[27]

These signs, through their scale, materiality, and language, are supposed to convey authority, assure us that here on this land *is history* and we are on the correct side of it. But at the same time, they are dirty, the markers wave in the wind, and they contain far too much text to be read while driving on a road where it's illegal to stop and read them. It's almost like the signs know they're just a bluff. More is at stake than just bad sculpture—how we memorialize our past says much about what we envision ourselves to be—they also feel utterly inconsequential.

Here, no Michael Brill–embodied landscape of granite thorns warns us of future and present danger, or reminds us of the lineage of displacement at SRS. (This line reaches out, far beyond South Carolina and the Savannah River and the South, to sustain the American war machine, dropping bomb after bomb to disappear towns not unlike Ellenton or Dunbarton. In doing so, the line profits companies like Bechtel and Lockheed Martin as they secure government contracts to contain the effects of the bombs they helped to build.) The markers do nothing to deter human intrusion. At best, they are false platitudes that ignore SRS's fraught history, from its effects on Black tenant farmers all the way up to the motivations for and repercussions of the arms race at the highest levels of government. At worst, they make sense of a story that never did.

Quantum physicist Karen Barad writes that when US forces dropped the first nuclear bomb on Hiroshima at 8:15 a.m. on August 6, 1945, "time died in a flash." Not only did the splitting of the atom reconfigure global-scale geopolitics and destroy entire cities, but it shattered nested notions of scale (building < neighborhood < city < state < nation) and anything like an ontological commitment to differentiating between "micro" and "macro." If an atom's tiny nucleus, one hundred thousand times smaller than the atom, a near nothingness, results in incalculable devastation and uncountable deaths, then any presupposed concept of scale is fully blown to bits. The nuclear flash, hands of time moving and no longer moving, lays bare that

**Field (after Brill)**, 2020. Ink on paper. Drawing by the author.

time is unstable, continually leaking away from itself. For Barad, "Each moment is a multiplicity within a given singularity. Time will never be the same — at least for the time-being."[28]

Instead of safeguards, what we get is an atomic *House*, the K Reactor surrounded by barbed wire and rubble, a fatalist reminder of what we lost in the throes of a nuclear psychosis, of the bed we made and now must lie in together. *House*, despite being a memorial to memory, was reduced to dust early because some thought it was monstrous. But the sculpture, although structurally stable, was inevitably always the pre-trembling of the fall itself. It was about loss, and so it was.

As we come to understand our current geological age, the Anthropocene, as a process-state at the edge of geo-history or, in other words, an always being-towards-death, the K Reactor is in its own pre-trembling. The flimsy aluminum historic signs, hard but ultimately hollow, only half-heartedly ask us to believe them. Together, they offer a solemn warning, but only if we know how to look for it. They certainly do not protect us, nor can they offer us an alternative to the ubiquity of violence. Their origin — a project of dispossession cloaked in patriotism — precludes that.

Maybe, though, the signs' hollowness, or their seemingly perpetual dampness, or the potentially radioactive lichen growing over their text, making and unmaking history and time, offer an argument against a temporal certainty. The emerging polemic is a defense of an un-knowing about what once was or is or might come next, not because of a position in an empire but in spite of it. A mutant ecology's own détournement. ◌

1   Édouard Glissant, *Poetics of Relation*, trans. Betsy Wing (Ann Arbor: University of Michigan Press, 1997), 209.

2   Doug Pardue, "Deadly Legacy: Savannah River Site Near Aiken One of the Most Contaminated Places on Earth," *Post and Courier*, May 21, 2017, https://www.postandcourier.com/news/deadly-legacy-savannah-river-site-near-aiken-one-of-the-most-contaminated-places-on-earth/article_d325f494-12ff-11e7-9579-6b0721ccae53.html; Gene Aloise, *Securing U.S. Nuclear Materials: DOE Needs to Take Action to Safely Consolidate Plutonium*, GAO-05-665 (Washington, DC: Government Accountability Office, 2005), 7; Robert Alvarez, "Plutonium Wastes from the U.S. Nuclear Weapons Complex," *Science & Global Security* 19, no. 1 (2011): 17–18.

3   Richard Shone, "Rachel Whiteread's 'House'. London," *Burlington Magazine* 135, no. 1089 (December 1993): 837.

4   Lucie Anne Genay, "The Scientific Conquest of New Mexico: Local Legacies of the Manhattan Project 1942–2015" (PhD diss., Université Stendhal Grenoble, 2015), 133.

5   Joseph Masco, "Mutant Ecologies: Radioactive Life in Post–Cold War New Mexico," *Cultural Anthropology* 19, no. 4 (November 2004): 530.

6   Pardue, "Deadly Legacy"; "Barnwell County, South Carolina; South Carolina," United States Census Bureau, July 1, 2019, https://www.census.gov/quickfacts/fact/table/barnwellcounty-southcarolina,SC/PST045219.

7   Charles Pinderhughes, "Toward a New Theory of Internal Colonialism," *Socialism and Democracy* 25, no. 1 (March 2011): 244.

8   Kari Frederickson, "Creating a 'Respectable Area': Southerners and the Cold War," *Diplomatic History* 36, no. 3 (June 2012): 488.

9   Frederickson, "Creating a 'Respectable Area,'" 488–489.

10  Janice Harper, "Secrets Revealed, Revelations Concealed: A Secret City Confronts Its Environmental Legacy of Weapons Production," *Anthropological Quarterly* 80, no. 1 (Winter 2007): 44–46.

11  Richard Seymour, "Cold War Anticommunism and the Defence of White Supremacy in the Southern United States" (PhD diss., London School of Economics and Political Science, 2016), 131.

12  Seymour, "Cold War Anticommunism," 10, 235, 8.

13  Thomas A. Sebeok, "Pandora's Box: How and Why to Communicate 10,000 Years into the Future," Media Arts and Technology, University of California Santa Barbara, accessed April 10, 2021, https://www.mat.ucsb.edu/~g.legrady/academic/courses/01sp200a/students/enricaLovaglio/pandora/Pandora.html.

14  Kathleen M. Trauth, Stephen C. Hora, and Robert V. Guzowski, *Expert Judgement on Markers to Deter Inadvertent Human Intrusion into the Waste Isolation Pilot Plant*, US Department of Energy & Sandia National Laboratories (Albuquerque, NM: US Department of Energy, 1993), F-57.

15  Masco, "Mutant Ecologies," 523.

16  Kate Brown, "Chernobyl Mono-Cropped," *RCC Perspectives*, no. 9 (2012): 53.

17  Loka Ashwood and Steve Wing, "Worker Alienation and Compensation at the Savannah River Site," *New Solutions: A Journal of Environmental and Occupational Health Policy* 26, no. 1 (2016): 60.

18  Kim A. Angelon-Gaetz, David B. Richardson, and Steve Wing, "Inequalities in the Nuclear Age: Impact of Race and Gender on Radiation Exposure at the Savannah River Site (1951–1999)," *New Solutions: A Journal of Environmental and Occupational Health Policy* 20, no. 2 (2010): 195.

19  Peter Coates, Tim Cole, Marianna Dudley, and Chris Pearson, "Defending Nation, Defending Nature? Militarized Landscapes and Military Environmentalism in Britain, France, and the United States," *Environmental History* 16, no. 3 (July 2011): 465–469.

20 "Par Pond, Upper 3 Runs Creek – Savannah River Site, South Carolina," SCIWAY, May 2009, https://www.sciway.net/srs-savannah-river-site/par-pond.html; Jennifer Gibbons, "Ecological Biodiversity on Savannah River Site Continues to Thrive," Odum School of Ecology, University of Georgia, July 18, 2011, https://www.ecology.uga.edu/ecological-biodiversity-on-savannah-river-site-continues-to-thrive/; *NPL Site Narrative for Savannah River Site (USDOE)* (Aiken, SC: US Department of Energy, 1991), 2.

21 Gibbons, "Ecological Biodiversity"; Andreas Huyssen, *Present Pasts: Urban Palimpsests and the Politics of Memory*, Cultural Memory in the Present (Stanford, CA: Stanford University Press, 2003), 28.

22 The first statewide programs to erect roadside historical markers began in the late 1920s, but the largest number of state-sponsored programs developed after World War II. In the decades following the war, American families took to highways on vacations, which had as much to do with recreation as it did with a desire to explore historic sites that reflected a patriotic national identity and forged a sense of good citizenship at the dawn of the Cold War. At the peak of America's cultural and political struggle against the Soviet Union, heritage tourism propagated narratives that catered to middle-class white America. The vast majority of historical markers reinforce themes of all-knowing Founding Fathers, American exceptionalism, brilliant and strategic soldiers, and brave settlers on a local level by foregrounding residents (mostly white and male) and events that point to shared values with these midtwentieth-century, white, middle-class travelers. In 1954 alone, around forty-nine million Americans set out on heritage tours of the United States. Kevin M. Levin, "When It Comes to Historical Markers, Every Word Matters," *Smithsonian Magazine*, July 6, 2017, https://www.smithsonianmag.com/history/when-it-comes-historical-markers-every-word-matters-180963973/.

23 "SRS History Highlights," Savannah River Site, US Department of Energy, accessed March 2, 2021, https://www.srs.gov/general/about/history1.htm.

24 "Discover Aiken: 10 S.C. Historical Markers to Know in Aiken County," *Aiken Standard*, last updated November 9, 2020, https://www.postandcourier.com/aikenstandard/news/discover/discover-aiken-10-s-c-historical-markers-to-know-in-aiken-county/article_27830560-0cb0-11eb-a4c5-4bb-13bc1c415.html.

25 Paul Sauerborn, "Cold War Historic Preservation Program," Savannah River Nuclear Solutions, LLC (PowerPoint presentation, SRS Citizens Advisory Board Strategic and Legacy Management Committee, June 14, 2011), https://cab.srs.gov/library/meetings/2011/slm/20110614_historicpreservation.pdf.

26 Samuel Ritchie, "That Others May Live: The Cold War Sacrifice of Ellenton, South Carolina" (master's thesis, Clemson University, 2009), 78.

27 Trauth, Hora, and Guzowski, *Expert Judgement on Markers*, F-57.

28 Karen Barad, "No Small Matter: Mushroom Clouds, Ecologies of Nothingness, and Strange Topologies of Spacetimemattering," in *Arts of Living on a Damaged Planet*, ed. Anna Tsing, Heather Swanson, Elaine Gan, and Nils Bubandt (Minneapolis: University of Minnesota Press, 2017), G106–G109.

**Tree**, May 2019.

# How to Build a Home

**W**HEN I WAS SIX YEARS OLD, my family and I packed up our life in four suitcases and left Sanming, my hometown, located in the western Fujian province of China. I didn't know where I was going, and my parents didn't know what they were expecting. All we knew was that we were moving to North Carolina to reunite with my paternal grandparents, who already resided in Durham. In 2003, we said goodbye to the only life that we'd known in order to achieve a dream that we'd heard about but never seen.

During our very first plane ride, I ended up locked in the bathroom twice because I couldn't figure out how to operate the folding door. I pressed the crimson red emergency button in panic, and I remember the terror on the flight attendant's face when she found me there. I had zero knowledge of English and was very shy, so I smiled and quickly ran back to my seat. Thankfully, I slept through most of the thirteen-hour flight to Raleigh-Durham.

My grandparents picked us up at the airport and it was my first time meeting them. They'd left China before I was born. There were a lot of new things to get used to, but warming up to my grandparents was the first. I spent a month with them at home before enrolling in school, while my parents immediately looked for work. My mother started working as a waitress in a Chinese restaurant, and my father learned home repair skills from my grandfather, eventually establishing his own business. My parents didn't know any English, so they attended ESL classes at UNC during their days off. At that time, I couldn't fully understand why they were always stressed and had a hard time learning the language. I was fluent in just a year and I immediately became the translator for our family. Being their translator led me into their world, and over

*by* Cici Cheng

the years I slowly began to realize how much they'd sacrificed and struggled because of the language barrier. I was required to grow up faster than other kids. I helped complete tasks for my parents, from filling out government forms to accompanying them at the DMV. Though the role of being a young translator was often nerve-racking, I wouldn't be the independent and intrepid woman I am today without that experience.

When I didn't have access to the school library, I read the home improvement books that my dad scattered around the house. Luckily, the books had plenty of illustrations. They were mostly images of toilet fill valve sets or steps for replacing light fixtures, but I took what I could get. I had been exposed to building repair work at a very young age since it was my dad and grandfather's occupation.

After leaving my childhood home in China, I struggled to feel attached to another place. The homes that we lived in merely provided a roof over our heads. There was a disconnect between those spaces and me because I felt that part of my identity had been left behind in China. I often had a hard time trying to make sense of where I truly belonged—where I could feel comfort—especially growing up in two different cultures.

Sixteen years later, I am experiencing that feeling again. In April 2019, my parents bought their very first home: a two-story 1970s contemporary on three-and-a-half wooded acres in Chapel Hill. It needed lots of TLC, but my father saw an opportunity. "If not now, then when?" he said. Here was a home that we could finally afford—better yet, that we could work together to make into our dream home. We envisioned a big porch, black spiral staircase, and maybe even a Toto toilet.

This is the home where we can imprint ourselves, our identities, our culture, our memories. While constructing different parts of the house, we are also starting to build the American Dream that my parents went searching for years ago. The process of working on this house together as a family has made me realize what I needed to become emotionally attached to a place. My family's indestructible bonds made this attachment possible, starting from when we got on a plane to the United States. Back then, all we had was each other. ◐

> **After leaving my childhood home in China, I struggled to feel attached to another place.** The homes that we lived in merely provided a roof over our heads.

**Fall**, October 2019. My brother stands in the middle of the driveway while the wind blows.

**Windows**, February 2020. My mother sands the window trims.

**Front Door**, August 2019. My father looks at his phone after breaking apart the porch.

**Spring**, April 2019.

**Laundry Room**, September 2019. My mother does laundry.

**Bathtub (Self-Portrait #1)**, January 2020.

**Stairs**, September 2019. The staircase next to what used to be the greenhouse.

**Back Porch**, January 2020. My father and our dog look across the property.

**Storage Room**, October 2019. My father and brother take a break.

**Living Room (Self-Portrait #2)**, November 2019.

**Shadow**, November 2019. My mother reflected in old windows.

**Work Bench**, April 2019.

**Dining Room**, May 2019. My mother sits on a beach chair.

# The Kinetic South

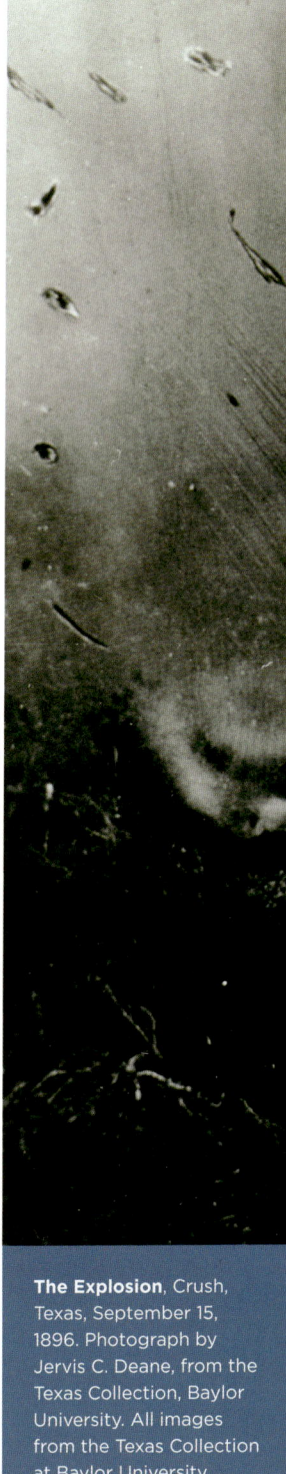

**I**T WAS NOT SUPPOSED TO end like this. On September 15, 1896, "Crush, Texas," was supposed to be just another kinetic spectacle in a place replete with them. The name was a double entendre, both a cheeky allusion to the staged head-on train collision scheduled to take place there and an eponym for William G. Crush, the Missouri–Kansas–Texas Railroad general passenger and ticket agent who devised it.

Nearby, Wacoans brimmed with excitement for the crash and devoured news about the "city of a day" built to host it. Disembarking at "Crush Station," an audience of as many as forty thousand people found every desire accounted for: a dining room and thirty vendors fed them, and bandstands, freak shows, and shooting galleries entertained them. Turn-of-the-century infrastructure, including two telegraph offices, running water, and a jail, gave airs of permanence and control.[1]

Shortly after 5:00 p.m., any pretense to order evaporated when the impact of the crash exploded the boilers of the two colliding engines. Pandemonium struck. Almost instantly, shrapnel leveled a dozen attendees, at least three of whom would die. The crowd, unfazed, rushed the wreck, dodging soaring debris to mount the cars and collect souvenirs from the wreckage. The frenzy fizzled fast. By 7:00 p.m., spectators like Maggie Dunn had returned to Waco, where they supped and "passed the time off very pleasantly" for hours. The rapid return to normalcy suggests that Crush was unusual but not exceptional. It was embedded within a thirty-five year history that produced a distinct sense of self and self-imagining in Waco — one where the kinetic spectacular was not only routine but foundational to the making of the New South.[2]

*by* Alex Hofmann

**The Explosion**, Crush, Texas, September 15, 1896. Photograph by Jervis C. Deane, from the Texas Collection, Baylor University. All images from the Texas Collection at Baylor University unless otherwise noted.

## New South Modernity

The "New South" was a slogan, a critique, a vision, a movement, a creed, a period—symbolic, hyperbolic, mythological. In its most limited sense, the New South was a *kintsugi* worldview forged from pieces of a shattered past. Humiliated by a doomed bid for a slaveholders' republic, boosters pedaled a model for an urbanized and industrialized South with diversified scientific agriculture. Despite their best efforts, however, the postbellum South continued to haunt the popular imagination as backward, prostrate, and stagnant. The oppressive climate seemed to demand it, the drawl articulate it, the poverty guarantee it. "Diseases of laziness"—hookworm and pellagra—besieged southern bodies from without and within. Another disease, unfettered capitalism, sapped what little energy those bodies had, as railroads and extractive industries created a parasitic economy where productivity soared and standards of living froze. In the decades after Appomattox, journalists, academics, reformers, and photographers went South and portrayed the region as "pre-modern," a reflexive vindication of the northern way of life.[3]

Modernity in the form of urbanization and industrialization would not arrive in the South until the New Deal and World War II. Yet, modernity is more than economics; it is an ensemble of (at times contradictory) technologies and ways of seeing the world. For this reason, C. Vann Woodward urged historians to search for a modernity rooted in a new southern sensibility. Recovering this requires stripping away expectations set by northern development and mores. Doing so brings into focus an endemic modern impulse to categorize, classify, and rationalize that extended to the rural corners of the New South. Modernity foregrounded the region's most repugnant rituals of Jim Crow, as white southerners spliced up their populations to regulate movements that threatened to undo the unstable racial regime.[4]

An additional aspect of modernity remains overlooked in studies of the New South: speed. After the Civil War, Americans mapped increasingly rapid cycles of destruction and creation onto their cultural and political landscape. Quickening motion—of technologies, of politics, of people—defined the age's aesthetic. This same obsession was evident in the South, where it took on a decidedly southern cadence. It can be difficult to see motion as a defining feature of the New South when focusing on the period's representative cities like Richmond, Charleston, and Atlanta. There, the omnipresent metaphor of springing back to life occludes the significance of literal motion in everyday existence. These damaged cities provided easy fodder for local boosters like Atlanta's Henry Grady, who tethered ideas of a "New" industrial and urban South to images of a phoenix-like rebirth from the war's ashes. Yet, as Woodward warned, urban boosters left a domineering presence in the archive that threatened to set historians' agendas, conflating the metaphors of their programs with the experiences of regular postbellum southerners. While historians have reappraised the New South as a period and way of life beyond boosterism—querying what it was like to live in this volatile era and how the Civil War set the trajectory of these developments—the settings and characters in these updated histories remain largely the same.[5]

Atlanta had a foil: Waco, Texas. Waco, too, was a postbellum tabula rasa—but of a different sort. One hundred miles from everywhere, in 1860, it was a small wooden village of eight hundred people that exploded after the Civil War to become a midsized city and capital of nineteenth-century spectacle. Untouched by war, Waco was free of the white noise of boosters and destruction. This remote western outpost of the New South illuminates how mobility was more than a booster metaphor for regional regeneration.[6]

**Cotton Palace Parade**, Waco, Texas, 1894.

Here, a kinetic South comes into view. The war forged a fascination with movement, structuring white Wacoans' perceptions of their natural, built, and social environments. The town teemed with motion for motion's sake, which white residents touted, performed, and guarded as a racialized privilege. Movement became an organizing principle of life underwriting a particular (and particularly raced) conception of a new, modern South. In this light, Crush was an extreme spectacle of motion that was at once crescendo and coda to thirty years of constructing and celebrating a kinetic South.

## Postbellum Migrations

With a population nearly 40 percent enslaved just four years after Waco's incorporation in 1856, secession was all but guaranteed, and at least 60 percent of Waco's white males enlisted. Despite strong ties to the Civil War, postbellum Waco had a weak Confederate culture. No monument ever adorned its square, and the United Daughters of the Confederacy (UDC)— elsewhere the midwives of memory—mustered little support. Unlike much of the former

Confederacy, Wacoans were not preoccupied by the war, though they were forever marked by it.[7]

A month before Appomattox, Waco's mayor Richard N. Goode could still truthfully state, "We have not suffered very materially yet." For soldiers and civilians of McLennan County, the shared Civil War experience was ennui. Via the lifeline of correspondence, soldiers and their families looked to each other for excitement neither could provide. When James Black lamented inaction, his wife responded, "You asked me to write all that takes place. Well, there is nothing interesting, funny, or dreadful occurring." The war did not cause mass suffering in Waco as much as it paused its development. Residents were aware of this, for it was the key to their postbellum boom.[8]

After the Civil War, the South suffered extreme economic and psychic malaise. As a whole, the region saw a 30 percent loss in property, and agriculture languished until 1900. Texas was the

Promotional pamphlet for the Texas Cotton Palace, 1894.

great exception. With few battles, no starvation, and little disease, Texas became the nation's premier postbellum cotton producer. A particularly weak Reconstruction made this fertile and pristine land all the more enticing for white southerners. Texas state politicians were adept at clearing the lowest bars of presidential and congressional Reconstruction while leaning on extreme racial violence to preempt any meaningful interracial politics. Nary a single Black politician rose to major office, and only fourteen joined the legislature. Regardless, President Ulysses S. Grant readmitted Texas to the Union in March 1870. After Democrats retook the governorship in 1874 under Waco lawyer, secession leader, and Confederate veteran Richard Coke, Reconstruction suffered a staggered death in the hands of omnipotent district judges overseeing local elections and appointments. As historian Carl H. Moneyhon noted, although Texas could have become anything between 1865 and 1874, it ended up a clone of its 1861 self: one-party rule over a cotton economy.[9]

McLennan County became a microcosm of these state trends. With limited wartime suffering, returning veterans resumed their studies, reopened shops, and replanted fields as if nothing had happened. By 1876, one city directory could proclaim that "as yet, 'cotton is king.'" The county bounced back so quickly that, looking back from 1893, another directory boasted,

"Whatever injury the war caused McLennan county her recuperative power was marvelous." The same was true psychically, as local politicians ended Reconstruction swiftly after Coke's election. As a result, McLennan County became one of many places in Texas where white southerners buckling under the weight of their historical choices could imagine starting anew on quasi-antebellum terms.[10]

State and county alike became a vast southern Eden for those ruined in war. Before Appomattox, white southerners delayed emancipation by fleeing to Texas to evade advancing Union lines. For them, this journey held promise; for the enslaved, anguish, as established kinship networks were destroyed. The radically different conditions of wartime resettlement set the trajectory for the future. White and Black population growth in Texas were near equal between 1860 and 1870. Afterward, hundreds of thousands of white southerners flocked to the one place where the distance between the Old and New Souths required no great cognitive leap. For the next two decades, Texas's white population increased at twice the rate as its Black counterpart, as white resettlement underwrote a population surge of more than 1.3 million white to just over 305,000 Black people between 1860 and 1890. These demographic shifts ensured that postbellum visions of Texas prosperity remained predominantly white. In all, Texas experienced an unparalleled 270 percent population growth from 1860 to 1890; McLennan County, 532 percent; and Waco, 380 percent. By 1880, Texas led all former Confederate states in number of residents born in another state, with 606,428 total. Eighty percent of these were from the Deep South.[11]

McLennan County's out-of-state population exceeded state patterns, topping 50 percent from 1870 to 1880. White Wacoans sacralized these shifts in the stories they told themselves. One UDC member recalled, "Waco was settled, chiefly after the Civil War, by people from the Southern States who had lost all their property through the War and came to the new land to build up their fortunes and establish new homes." This was not Confederate mythmaking. Many veterans briefly returned home only to abandon their desolate land and start over in Waco's cotton industry. Here arose a paradox: white southerners migrated for continuity, yet the extraordinary demographic changes they effected brought about a radical break with the past.[12]

## Cotton's Mobile Kingdom

The war set off a movement of peoples, machinery, technology, and products that would structure postbellum Wacoans' perceptions, values, and self-imaginings for the next fifty years. Migration and development spurred each other in quickening succession. Once the Chisholm Trail provided immediate cash flow, white Wacoans rapidly ticked off all the markers of development: a bridge connecting Waco's two halves split by the Brazos River; the telegraph facilitating a cotton economy; and a railroad by 1873. These developments and attendant mass migrations embedded movement as the cornerstone of their postbellum city in the white Waco imagination.[13]

As Wacoans predicated progress and prosperity on kinetics, the movement of peoples became the great wonder of McLennan County. In 1894, Wacoans built a shrine not just to cotton but to the movement it incited. Inspired by the Midwest Corn Palace, businessman J. W. Riggins and his Waco Commercial Club capitalized upon Texas's domination of the cotton industry to launch a Cotton Palace. The project had two functions. First, it attracted more attention, respect, migrants, and industry to Waco by providing "a photograph in miniature, as it were, of the capabilities of soil and climate." Unlike fairs, which haphazardly displayed sample harvests, the palace cloaked the building's very infrastructure in cotton. This quite literally suggested cotton was the foundation, pillars, and shelter for their society.[14]

Yet the Cotton Palace doubled as a story white Wacoans told themselves. Through themed performative narratives, the Cotton Palace allowed Wacoans to commemorate the historical migrations that produced their booming city. This was not remembrance so much as a twenty-nine-day performance. Riggins promised a deeper appreciation of cotton's role in Texas through "a grand cotton jubilee, upon which occasion King Cotton shall be crowned king, and enthroned in an appropriate place." It would commemorate the coming of peoples to till the land at the hand of King Cotton.[15]

Riggins referred to it as a "grand King Cotton Carnival" in the medieval sense: a pageant laden with symbolism. The Cotton Palace opened with a parade on November 8, 1894. Streamers coated every building in Waco, "waiving [sic] a welcome to the monarch Cotton" personified, who led thirty thousand people from city hall to the baroque, quarter-million-dollar Cotton Palace. Wacoans repeated this pageantry daily. Organizers assigned a theme to each day that celebrated a particular demographic prominent in Waco's past and present—including laborers, railroad workers, cowboys, bicyclists, and more—by giving them their own parade. As a result, every day, a particular group made its pilgrimage to pay tithe and tribute to what brought them to Texas: King Cotton. In the streets, white Wacoans manifested their perceptions of the literal movement that developed their city.[16]

Black Wacoans wanted little to do with it. A special "Negro Day" had lackluster attendance. After all, Black Wacoans had a different historical experience with mobility that began with forced wartime migrations with their enslavers. In the 1890s, white Texans continued to vie for control of Black Texans' movements. The particularities of Jim Crow in Waco remain unwritten, but there is no reason to believe the city was exceptional. Legal segregation began in Texas in 1891. As elsewhere, it was no coincidence that it originated with trains, which tethered together ideas of physical and social mobility in the New South. Movement threatened a Jim Crow regime reliant on improvisation and custom as much as statute. The eponymous minstrel character was a traveler, significant in that Black Americans long understood citizenship as the inverse of their condition: unfettered movement. They would not find that in Waco. When they could break free and move, for many it would be with intention, away from the South during the Great Migration.[17]

Nothing captured the racialized privileges of movement more than the booming success of "Planter's Day" that seemed a rebuttal of "Negro Day" in its celebration of Black Wacoans' oppressors. The press described a late-night "Harvest Carnival Ball" that followed a parade adorned with $100,000 worth of cotton. The ball "opened with a grand allegorical march symbolizing the pursuit and progress of agriculture from the sowing of the seed to the reaping of the harvest, and the consequent wealth produced thereby for the glory of Texas." Ceres, Roman goddess of agriculture, watched the procession from the five thousand–seat auditorium to the exhibition hall. Goddesses Flora, Harvest, Fruit, Texas, and Fortune marched with corresponding seasons and laborers. At the end, Ceres declared Cotton king and wed him to "Goddess Texas."[18]

Inside the palace, visitors explored one hundred thousand square feet of cotton-related exhibits across two floors. Upstairs, women used local crops to create eighteen scenes of fantasy, mythology, and history. These carried no overarching narrative, which, paradoxically, imparted their meaning. Waco's newspaper *Artesia* reported, "The combination of the beautiful with the historical; the mythological with the allegorical, forms a very pleasing transition." Having these dioramas encircle King Cotton and Ceres melded disparate images into a tableau thematically united by the raw material comprising them. Cotton sat on a throne among his royal court. Nearby, Ceres looked down upon a miniature Cotton Palace that gave her offerings. Beneath Ceres, a floor map of Texas made from cotton and seed portrayed "Waco's being the center and the only spot in Texas, the nucleus for all the railroads and the head of the Brazos navigation." Together, the scenes were a reminder that Ceres and King Cotton gave Wacoans everything—and made Waco the mobile hub of Texas. In daily marches to the Cotton Palace and activities within it, white Wacoans reenacted this historical development in a kind of double pilgrimage.[19]

## Waco Wellspring

This same preoccupation with motion structured perceptions of everyday life, including Waco's geography. When former miner Joseph Daniel Bell tapped the city's first artesian well in March 1886, he set off a frenzy. Wacoans discovered that they lived atop a reservoir and created twenty-five wells, producing up to one million gallons of water daily. Wacoans obsessed over measuring the power of these reservoirs. An 1893 directory boasted that these "marvels of Waco" were commonly called geysers, "owing to the fact that the water is ejected at a pressure of 67 pounds to the square inch" from "a 100-foot standpipe, with a capacity of 175,000 gallons. Through an inch and a quarter ring nozzle this water can be thrown 108 feet vertically." This made for rich imagery and even richer uses: to Wacoans' delight, the wells powered machinery and elevators and flushed gutters.[20]

Wells also filled natatoriums, where white Wacoans perceived the movement of water and

people as curative. Padgett's Park Natatorium featured twenty-four bathrooms with porcelain tubs, a dozen vapor baths, two needle baths, electric and Russian baths, and a sweating and cooling room. The Natatorio-Sanatorium, Padgett's rival, was a seven-floored palace boasting the same plus cold plunges and needle baths that ostensibly healed through pressurized jets. In pools, swimmers did laps, went down slides, and used gymnastic equipment like hanging rings and ropes. Because the pressure and speed of water alternated—and Wacoans exercised in it—the city became a healing center of the world. By one estimate, "hundreds of invalids, nay thousands, have flocked thither, got relief of their aliments, [and] hung up their crutches for monuments." Attributing its alleged "lowest death rate in Texas" to "God's gifts to Waco," promoters challenged its white patrons to leave unhealed.[21]

As white Wacoans marveled at the kinetic properties of wells, they mapped them onto their social geography as well. Isaac Goldstein founded the society paper *Gossip* in November 1892. Months later, he rechristened it *Artesia* to promote Waco's wells. The name reflected his "hopes to be as clear in its delineation of facts as the pool of Bethesda, and as replete with healing for those afflicted with ennui." As with wells, the paper measured, monitored, and celebrated the movement of people. This four-page weekly dedicated itself to covering the

fashion, parties, gossip, and activities of Wacoans. At least the final half page always tracked people's movements to and from the city. Where they went and for how long was a constant subject of public comment and concern. For this very reason, local provocateur and publisher William Cowper Brann suggested "Meddlerville" would be a better name for the city. Brann elaborated, "Of our 30,000 inhabitants fully one-third have an idea that heaven is an eternity of keyholes and that angels have more eyes than Argos."[22]

Frenetic energy poured from the earth into the streets. Ever since the Bicycle Club formed in 1892 and convinced businessman Tom Padgett to build a racetrack, bicycling seemed an unstoppable mania. The "bicyclius" had become a "pandemic," Brann observed. "The landscape is literally alive with whirling wheels and churning legs—legs of all kinds, colors, classes and conditions." Wacoans aestheticized movement, turning it into an opportunity for social spectacle. "It was a beautiful sight from the stand to witness the wheelmen, gaily attired, spinning around the track on their glittering wheels," *Artesia* reported. By 1885, bike races pairing bicyclists against each other, roller-skaters, and horses became a popular feature of social life. Marveling at their relative speeds, these races became "a social affair of importance" marked with elaborate parades that rivaled the Columbian Exposition.[23]

**Shaking Hands**, Crush, Texas, September 15, 1896. Photograph by Jervis C. Deane.

When white women took up bicycling, public reaction underscored that unfettered movement was a right of white men only. Debate over the perils of women-on-wheels was not unique to Waco, but it turned on a different axis. All outrage over women cycling came down to fear over the independence the bicycle offered them. Nevertheless, the form that discourse took varied. Beyond Waco, Americans framed the debate in terms of the physical and moral damage the bicycle would cause. Wacoans, on the other hand, were clear that their protest had little to do with sex or injury and everything to do with how women moved in the presence of men. *Waco News* observed that the bicycle had a woman "working her limbs like a convict in a treadmill." They should be horseback riding instead. The latter was "graceful," the former, "ridiculous."[24]

William Cowper Brann honed this view. Unlike those claiming bicycles created infertile prostitutes, he dismissed the bike as sheer fad unrelated to morality. It was offensive because it made women move in all the wrong ways: "The wheel is the enemy of female beauty, and beauty is my religion." They went too fast, disrupting their natural harmony by becoming "a blot on the landscape." All men really wanted was "to forget that lovely woman has legs, to resume our adoration of the mysterious." Walking made woman "a perfect symphony" demon-

strating "the poetry of motion" rather than "an ungraceful trunk equipped with sprawling legs that awkwardly churn the atmosphere." (White) women were too good, too pure, and too harmonious for violent speed.[25]

Form aside, movement in and of itself remained a sacred right for white men and women alike. Its significance is revealed in the inverse: the restriction of movement for social outcasts. By authority of its new charter, Waco legalized prostitution in 1871. From the start, the sin was not one of commission but of visibility. Residents immediately lobbied politicians to "banish the women from the sidewalks in daylight" and perhaps across the Brazos River. In 1889, Mayor Champe McCulloch crafted a two-part solution that would at once eliminate prostitutes' visibility to the public and increase it to the state. First, Waco rezoned buildings between Jefferson Avenue, Washington Avenue, Two Street, and the Brazos River to contain legalized prostitution. Second, quarterly city licenses and bimonthly county medical exams formed a register of prostitutes to surveil them. What seemed like generic Progressive Era containment and regulation took on a particularly cruel hue in a place that perceived movement as a life-affirming privilege, and confinement as death.[26]

Carceral rhetoric underscored the point. Wacoans named this legal zone the "Reservation." Racial overtones aside, it implied women could not leave, a message that newspapers reaffirmed in references to prostitutes as "inmate[s] of the Reservation." It was a designation given to anyone living within its bounds until proven otherwise, as in one 1892 police court case that legally established a pianist and housekeeper as "residents" rather than inmates after finding no proof of sex work. Inmates who ventured outside the Reservation became "vagrants"—"a polite name for prostitution," according to *Waco Evening News*. If they wanted to buy provisions in town, they had to hire messengers or a city hack to take them to stores after hours. Some storeowners barred prostitutes from entering and instead sold wares through a curtain in the hack. For men, the Reservation was a permeable boundary; for women, to enter the Reservation was to pass through the veil, never to return.[27]

Migration, wells, bicycles, prostitution—these were just a few of the everyday kinetic spectacles white Wacoans imagined, scrutinized, and framed in terms of motion. This was the world Wacoans had built around movement, and in 1896, the Crash at Crush escalated their obsession.

## The Crash at Crush

The Missouri–Kansas–Texas Railroad (also known as "the Katy") had a storied career in Texas as the first railway connecting the state to the North in 1872. A decade later, it reached Waco, joining four other lines. When agent William Crush pitched the idea for the Crash at Crush, his motive was obvious: drum up business by selling excursion fares for the spectacle.[28]

Less clear was his inspiration. Perhaps Crush heard about traveling salesman Alfred Streeter's staged collisions months prior in the Midwest. Streeter used the spectacle to act out the great political battles of the day, labeling opposing engines with "McKinley" and "Bryan" or "Gold Standard" and "Free Silver." Perhaps Crush drew inspiration from crowds flocking to a train accident he witnessed. Or, perhaps it was an attempted morality play. There was no clearer symbol of the junction of modernity, speed, and the New South than railroads. With 90 percent of southern counties containing a railroad by 1890, they were the consummate tangible symbol of laissez fare capitalism. They were also the most dangerous, embodying risk on fiscal and personal levels. A controlled wreck could paradoxically reassure passengers fearful for their safety.[29]

Whatever Crush's inspiration, the stunt took on its own meaning within the broader context of Waco. Waco both qualified and heightened historian Wolfgang Schivelbusch's finding that the train created a vision of the world in motion. Wacoans shared this vision, but it originated in the prior thirty years of city growth. The train was merely symptomatic, Crush its logical conclusion.[30]

Once the Katy approved Crush's scheme, Crush and Waco's local agent scouted a site over two days in August 1896. Fourteen miles north of Waco, the spot chose them. A "natural amphitheater" would allow the trains to run north to south while spectators watched atop a plateau to the west. A 2 percent grade would funnel the trains into each other.[31]

Waco buzzed with anticipation. The sheer kinetics of the spectacle captured imaginations. In the streets, "Most people quit talking politics a few days ago and took up the subject of head-end collisions." In anticipation, Wacoans acted out the collision with their bodies. The *Houston Post* reported, "Not infrequently could be seen an earnest looking citizen plodding along the sidewalk muttering in an undertone, and presently he would jab his right fist into the palm of his left hand and you would know that he had witnessed a collision—in his mind."[32]

Even before the crash, journalists fixated on speed. The *Dallas Morning News* had joined Katy officials for test runs to locate the precise point of collision. "She moved off very slowly, but in two seconds was rushing along," the journalist marveled, "and in half a minute was going like the wind, and all the boys had to hold on hard to keep from being shaken off." The following day, the Katy ran another test "for the entertainment of the crowd," members of which could "see for themselves just how these engines can run." These were early indications that Crush was less about a spectacle of ruin than one of movement.[33]

The unfolding event was sublime. When attendees described it, they focused less on death and destruction than on the kinetics of it all: of resources, trains, and people. On September 15, 1896, thousands of Texans hopped on trains, seduced by the promise of movement on display on an unseen scale. At 3:00 p.m., the two trains arrived to raucous cheers. The Katy had them renumbered and repainted in bright green, yellow, blue, and "vermillion to add life to the effect." They were painted "gaudy and gay" to streak against nature as they careened towards each other. At 5:00 p.m., the collision began with the trains "shaking hands" before reversing to their starting points. Ten minutes later, their crews counted sixteen puffs, tied down the whistles, and jumped to safety. The movement was awesome, powerful, and intoxicating. Papers recreated the rush of the crash—detailed it, drew it out, suspended it forever in motion. "They rolled down a frightful rate of speed to within a quarter of a mile of each other. . . . Now they were within ten feet of each other." Then: the crash.[34]

Contrary to one prediction, there was no detailed "autopsy" on the wreck, nor any talk of it being "more ghastly than that of scattered lights, livers, brains, and viscera on the ten-story buildings of Chicago." Instead, spectators gawked at the kinetics involved. "Imagine," the *Houston Post* beckoned, "a force of 175 tons, or 350,000 pounds, going at the rate of ninety miles an hour, striking an immovable body. The result can never be described. Words bend and break in the attempt to record on paper the pictures on the mind, or the impression of the eye." Still, the press tried its best to capture the speed for readers. *Dallas Morning News* reported, "A crash, a sound of timbers rent and torn, and then a shower of splinters. . . . Both boilers exploded simultaneously and the air was filled with flying missiles of iron and steel varying in size from a postage stamp to half of a driving wheel, falling indiscriminately on the just and unjust."[35]

The crowd was "awe-stricken." As debris showered over them, journalists tracked their trajectories. Smokestacks and pieces of boilers "sailed" a quarter mile. Two one-ton trucks flew one hundred feet high, bulldozing a telegraph post. A driving wheel "sizzled and screamed, cutting its way through space with the speed of a shell." Brake chains twisted "like a serpent." Then, "The heavens had opened and emitted millions of undistinguishable pieces of iron and steel. . . . They had the speed of a bullet, and being larger in size were more destructive." The trains' energy seemed to transfer to the crowd. Belting a "united yell," attendees ripped apart wooden fences to charge the wreck and seize souvenirs. One reporter concluded, "The crowd seemed to be indifferent as to the catastrophe."[36]

Crush became a turning point in Waco's perceptions of motion. For some, movement—once redemptive—was now uncontrollable and traumatic. As simulacra, it was fine, but now, the Katy's chief clerk claimed, "It was too realistic to be comfortable." It left some unable to hear or look at trains without recoiling. Three decades of celebrating movement and increasing speed led to this—and some did not like what they saw.[37]

For most, though, Crush was a bona fide triumph. Death and mutilation paled in compar-

ison to the excitement of bodies in motion. One paper called it "a howling success." After all, "The trains performed perfectly." Another wrote that despite "its sad feature . . . the collision was superb, awe-inspiring in the extreme and grand in sublimity." Afterward, one attendee penned an illuminating letter to the *Austin Daily Statesman* explaining how Crush could be a success not in spite of tragedy but because of it:

> Why, I would shut up the Iliad, and let Hector and Achilles and all the gods and goddesses of the beautiful Grecian Mythology fight it out, while I watched those Iron Titans rushing and roaring along the plain to meet in one grand concussion, where sight and sound, form and motion, merged and was lost in one grand uproar, and from out of the cloud of smoke and steam rained down a shower of iron and wooden missiles.

He had come to see "pure material bodies" in motion and Crush more than delivered. This was a process to marvel at, not a travesty to scrutinize.[38]

In this respect, Crush was clarifying. From then on, Wacoans doubled down on celebrating movement for movement's sake. Artists glorified the event as the supreme kinetic spectacle. Jervis Deane — "leading photographer of Waco" — won photography rights from the Katy. Afterward, he and his brothers published at least six large photos of the collision. The first two

depicted Crush beforehand. The third, *The Trains Just as They Struck*, captured the two locomotives as blurry streaks immediately before colliding. It was a breathtaking image, not for its ability to freeze a moment but rather for its suspension of the trains in perpetual motion. The trains' advertisements were blurry, the engines appeared to melt, and the smoke trails look as if thickened and smeared with a brush. The juxtaposition of the crisp stillness of the foreground heightened the effect. Finally, *The Explosion*. Again, the photo drew attention to the left, where an amorphous burst of energy erupted, set against the tranquility of an undamaged end of one of the trains. The point was not to capture a pristine moment but an infinitely unfolding explosion, shrapnel flying to all parts of the frame. Like the articles describing the event, *Before the Crowd Got to the Wreck* focuses not on the ruins situated in the far left of the photo but rather the blurry masses sprinting toward the trains for souvenirs. Separately, these photos underscored the speed of each individual act of the event; together, they provided a zoetrope of motion — an animated loop in the viewer's mind of the movements surrounding the crash. It was a work of art that captured and celebrated the kinetics of it all.[39]

Crush entered other media in similar ways. Early in his career, Black pianist Scott Joplin was on tour with his Texas Medley Quartette in 1896 when he found a publisher in Temple, thirty miles south of Waco. One month after Crush, Joplin published his third piece of music that broke the mold: *Great Crush Collision March*, a sonic reenactment of the crash "dedicated to M. K. & T. Ry." The march began daintily, conjuring images of merriment in Crush before the stunt. Launching into the march's "trio," the song defied the march form. After a series of foreboding chords, Joplin entered a run of bass notes accompanied by low octave treble chords played fortissimo. "The noise of the trains while running the rate of sixty miles per hour," he annotated. Then, discords in a high octave, played with syncopating grace notes. "Whistling for the crossing," he noted. Another bass run: "Noise of the trains." More syncopated discords but with fewer beats and more urgency. "Whistle before the collision." Hands careening up and down the black and white trestles of the keyboard, they finally crash on a chord at the lowest end of the register. "The collision," Joplin noted, played fortissimo with the pedal and suspended with a fermata, instructing musicians to hold the chord as long as desired for dramatic effect. Joplin then returned to the gentler open of the march. Scholars have criticized the piece for ending anticlimactically, but what they deemed a failure may actually be Joplin's profound understanding of how white Wacoans responded to violent movement: by a quick return to normalcy. Because it utilized syncopation — a kind of melodic violence — for the first time, musicologist Rudi Blesh raised the possibility that this song was the origin of ragtime itself. Perhaps an understanding of kinetics and violence in the white South armed Joplin with a new way of conceptualizing music.[40]

Both Deane's and Joplin's works were stunning multisensory celebrations of violent speed. Other artists, like photographer Fred Gildersleeve — Deane's heir apparent — followed suit, pioneering aerial photography and documenting speed, machinery, and motion around Waco into World War I. Over a decade before a car crash inspired Italian poet Filippo Tommaso Martinelli to draft a futurist vision of a fast, destructive modernity, white Wacoans became futurists themselves. It was a vision inspired by war, reified through banalities of urban life, codified in its exclusion of and violence toward women and people of color, and exaggerated in Crush.

The following week did not slow down. *Artesia* reflected on a series of bike races, dances, a circus, a fashion bazaar, a Young Men's Christian Association party, and "a succession of lesser contrasts to make up a week of as truly Bohemian living as one could demand." Then there were the normal kinetic spectacles: "An afternoon canter, a spin on the bike, a turn on the drives, or a swim in the pool — they have all come within the past week as adjuncts to the more potent allurements for enjoyment." The columnist maligned the circus's quality, but that was hardly the point. "One goes for the frolic, not the performance."[41]

After Crush, Brann ridiculed J. B. Cranfill, one of his regular enemies and editor of the *Baptist Standard*, who criticized the collision. "In his mind's eye he sees buildings burned; whole hecatombs of bleating animals roasted, a man fricasseed alive at fifty cents admission, the Katy running excursion trains to all these horrors and filling its coffers with cash by wrecking the car of progress, telescoping civilization." Cranfill may have been onto something. Perhaps he sensed the dreadful ends that sacralized anarchic motion could — and would — bring, climaxing with the 1916 spectacle lynching of Jesse Washington, which Gildersleeve photographed in piecemeal blurry fashion as a perpetually unfolding process of destruction rather than the typical postmortem record.[42]

The New South pulsed with movement, and Waco was no exception. Other cities also created expositions, rode bicycles, and advertised their natural resources to invite immigration after the Civil War. Yet, casting out to the margins of the New South, free of the interference generated by war and boosterism, Waco makes clear what places like Atlanta obscure: this was not regeneration, it was an unleashing of kinetic energy, regardless of the form it took. The Civil War profoundly reoriented white southerners' perceptions of the material world. They became lay cultural theorists in myriad ways, one of which was embedding speed and mobility within everyday life. Progress suffered an endless array of mobile metaphors, but in the wake of the Civil War's destruction and dislocations, it was literal. A marvel, a tragedy. ◐

NOTES

1   Austin C. Rogers, "A Pre-Arranged Head End Collision," in *The Cosmopolitan: A Monthly Illustrated Magazine November 1896–April 1897*, vol. 22 (Irvington, NY: Cosmopolitan Press, 1897), 125, 129; "They Are All Ready," *Dallas Morning News*, September 14, 1896; "Railroad Matters," *Dallas Morning News*, September 13, 1896; "Stand at Crush Station," *Democrat* (McKinney, TX), September 10, 1896; "Scene of the Collision," *Dallas Morning News*, September 16, 1896; "Taking Care of the Crowds," *Dallas Morning News*, September 16, 1896; "Railroad Matters. The Katy's Grand Scientific Show of a Collision Between Two Trains," *Dallas Morning News*, August 13, 1896; "Railroad Matters," *Dallas Morning News*, September 12, 1896; "Dallas Well Represented," *Dallas Morning News*, September 16, 1896; "Is Over at Last," *Dallas Morning News*, September 16, 1896; John Banta, "Railroad Publicity Stunt Ended in Tragic Explosion," January 23, 1983, box 9, folder 5, Thomas E. Turner Sr. Papers, accession #2200, Texas Collection, Baylor University (hereafter cited as Texas Collection).

2   "They Are All Ready"; Letter, Maggie Dunn to W. H. Clift, September 16, 1896, box 246, folder 20, Crush Collision Collection, accession #1253, Texas Collection. Crush remains remarkably understudied. Extant literature ranges between reading Crush as economic escapism and a physical manifestation of high and low culture wars. See Mike Cox, *Train Crash at Crush, Texas: America's Deadliest Publicity Stunt* (Charleston, SC: History Press, 2019), 27; and Nancy Bentley, *Frantic Panoramas: American Literature and Mass Culture, 1870–1920* (Philadelphia: University of Pennsylvania Press, 2009), 1–4. Despite varying interpretations, all project modern astonishment onto the Crush collision and treat it as an anomalous event. By "kinetic spectacular," I mean events that captured the attention of masses and traded on movement.

3   Paul M. Gaston, *The New South Creed: A Study in Southern Mythmaking* (New York: Vintage Books, 1973), 7, 54, 92–93, 121–132, 162–163. Regarding pellagra, see Jack Temple Kirby, *Mockingbird Song: Ecological Landscapes of the South* (Chapel Hill: University of North Carolina Press, 2006), 203–210. For hookworm, see John Ettling, *The Germ of Laziness: Rockefeller Philanthropy and Public Health in the New South* (Cambridge, MA: Harvard University Press, 1981). On poverty and the wealth gap in the New South, see Gaston, *New South Creed*, 45–47; and Edward L. Ayers, *The Promise of the New South: Life After Reconstruction* (New York: Oxford University Press, 2007), 22. For how the South got its public image as backward and antimodern, see Scott L. Matthews, *Capturing the South: Imagining America's Most Documented Region* (Chapel Hill: University of North Carolina Press, 2018); and Natalie J. Ring, *The Problem South: Region, Empire, and the New Liberal State, 1880–1930* (Athens: University of Georgia Press, 2012).

4   C. Vann Woodward, *The Origins of the New South, 1877–1913* (Baton Rouge: Louisiana State University Press, 1993), 140–141; James C. Cobb, *Redefining Southern Culture: Mind & Identity in the Modern South* (Athens: University of Georgia Press, 1999), 2. Prominent texts on the late economic development of the South include Gavin Wright, *Old South, New South: Revolutions in the Southern Economy since the Civil War* (Baton Rouge: Louisiana State University Press, 1986); and Bruce J. Schulman, *From Cotton Belt to Sunbelt: Federal Policy, Economic Development, and the Transformation of the South, 1938–1980* (New York: Oxford University Press, 1991). On southern modernity, see Benjamin S. Child, *The Whole Machinery: The Rural Modern in Cultures of the U.S. South, 1890–1946* (Athens: University of Georgia Press, 2019); Grace Elizabeth Hale, *Making Whiteness: The Culture of Segregation in the South, 1890–1940* (New York: First Vintage Books, 1999); and Charles Postel, *The Populist Vision* (New York: Oxford University Press, 2007).

5   Marshall Berman, *All That Is Solid Melts into Air: The Experience of Modernity* (New York: Penguin Books, 1988), 288; Jackson Lears, *Rebirth of a Nation: The Making of Modern America, 1877–1920* (New York: HarperCollins, 2009), 1–9; William A. Link, *Atlanta, Cradle of the New South: Race and Remembering in the Civil War's Aftermath* (Chapel Hill: University of North Carolina Press, 2013), 33–34, 55–58; Woodward, *Origins of the New South*, ix. On the influence of technology on perceptions, see Wolfgang Schivelbusch, *The Railway Journey: The Industrialization of Time and Space in the Nineteenth*

*Century* (Oakland: University of California Press, 2014). On speed, power, and the modern state, see Paul Virilio, *Speed and Politics: An Essay on Dromology*, trans. Mark Polizzotti (New York: Semiotex(e), 1986). On the impact of speed on American and European aesthetics, see Hillel Schwartz, "Torque: The New Kinaesthetic of the 20th Century," in *Incorporations*, ed. Jonathan Crary and Sanford Kwinter (New York: Zone Books, 1992). For examinations of the texture of everyday life in the New South, see Ayers, *Promise of the New South*, vii–ix. On the relation between Civil War destruction and New South development, see Link, *Atlanta*, 3.

6 Waco occupied a unique regional position as both South and West. Given its historical ancestry, wartime experience, segregation, and cotton culture ranging from plantation to sharecropping, Waco was predominantly southern until at least the 1920s, when the demographics and scale of agriculture shifted toward a western model of ranches and Mexican labor. See Neil Foley, *The White Scourge: Mexicans, Blacks, and Poor Whites in Texas Cotton Culture* (Berkeley: University of California Press, 1999), 2–5.

7 In 1860, McLennan County contained 6,206 white and enslaved people. While deaths and later enlistments make the actual number unknowable, the most reliable estimate was that 1,200 white men were of eligible age for service (16–45) and that 1,300 served. Harold B. Simpson, *Gaines' Mill to Appomattox: Waco & McLennan County in Hood's Texas Brigade* (Waco, TX: Texian Press, 1963), 30. Waco's disinterest in Confederate memorialization is all the more shocking considering Texas had the highest per capita and whole numbers of surviving Confederate veterans in 1890. Of the 432,020 Confederate veterans living in the United States, 66,791 lived in Texas. These comprised 2.99 percent of the state's population. Virginia—the crucible of Confederate memory—was its closest rival, with veterans comprising 2.94 percent of the population. *Eleventh Census of the United States, 1890*, vol. 1 (Washington, DC: Government Printing Office, 1897), 804–806. While there is a Confederate monument in Waco's Oakwood Cemetery, this structure served a different purpose than the Confederate monuments placed in central public spaces. See Karen L. Cox, *Dixie's Daughters: The Daughters of the Confederacy and the Preservation of Confederate Culture* (Gainesville: University Press of Florida, 2003), 66–67. After its founding in 1887, Waco's Pat Cleburne Camp of the United Confederate Veterans rarely drew more than 150 members. *Morrison & Fourmy's General Directory of the City of Waco, 1888–89* (Galveston, TX: Morrison & Fourmy, 1889), 47. The UDC had only twenty-five members when organized in 1894. *Morrison & Fourmy's General Directory of the City of Waco, 1894–95* (Galveston, TX: Morrison & Fourmy, 1895), 59.

8 Letter, R. N. Goode to Mary Virginia Thompson, March 19, 1865, box 1, folder 3, Goode-Thompson Family Papers, 1837–1993, accession #2794, series II: Richard N. Goode, Texas Collection; Letter, Patience Crain Black to James Black, June 17, 1862, in *A Copy of the Letters of Patience and James Black (1862–1865): Their Correspondence while Separated by the Civil War* (1972), 39.

9 Eric Foner, *Reconstruction: America's Unfinished Revolution: 1863–1877* (New York: HarperCollins, 2005), 125, 119, 204, 352–354; Roger L. Ransom and Richard Sutch, *One Kind of Freedom: The Economic Consequences of Emancipation*, 2nd ed. (New York: Cambridge University Press, 2001), 41–42, 171; Foley, *White Scourge*, 28; Charles William Ramsdell, "Reconstruction in Texas," in *History of Texas Democracy: A Centennial History of Politics and Personalities of the Democratic Party, 1836–1936*, ed. Frank Carter Adams (Austin, TX: Democratic Historical Association), 1: 237; Patrick G. Williams, *Beyond Redemption: Texas Democrats after Reconstruction* (College Station: Texas A&M University Press, 2007), 15–16, 55–60; Carl H. Moneyhon, *Texas after the Civil War: The Struggle of Reconstruction* (College Station: Texas A&M University Press, 2004), 3. Economists Ransom and Sutch argued that the region's straggling economy resulted from the loss of enslaved labor, not physical destruction. Ransom and Sutch, *One Kind of Freedom*, 50. Whether or not the Civil War's desolation was to blame was irrelevant, for white southerners felt it was. It was this perception that triggered a massive demographic shift.

10 John Sleeper and J. C. Hutchins, *Waco and McLennan County, Texas* (Waco, TX: Examined Steam Job Establishment, 1876), 26; *A Memorial and Biographical History of McLennan, Falls, Bell, and Coryell*

*Counties, Texas* (Chicago: 1893), University of North Texas Libraries, The Portal to Texas History, 47–48, 121; "Reconstruction in McLennan County," in *The Handbook of Waco and McLennan County, Texas*, ed. Dayton Kelly (Waco, TX: Texian Press, 1972), 221. For representative individual examples of Confederate veterans in Texas's postwar economy, see "Forsgard, Samuel J.," "Johnson, Charles L.," and "Makeig, Stephen L.," in *The Handbook of Waco and McLennan County, Texas*, ed. Dayton Kelly (Waco, TX: Texian Press, 1972), 104, 143, 178; and *Memorial and Biographical History*, 543, 725–726.

11 Leon F. Litwack, *Been in the Storm So Long: The Aftermath of Slavery* (New York: Vintage Books, 1980), 30–33; *Eleventh Census*, 400; Ralph A. Wooster, *Civil War Texas: A History and a Guide* (Austin, TX: Texas State Historical Association, 1999), 32, 45. Only Arkansas and Florida topped 100 percent growth between 1860 and 1890. Williams, *Beyond Redemption*, 4. After Texas, the ex-Confederate state with the most residents born out of state was Arkansas with 355,498 people. *Tenth Census of the United States, 1880*, vol. 1 (Washington, DC: Government Printing Office, 1883), 480. Texas was the most popular destination for emigrants from Alabama, Mississippi, Louisiana, and Arkansas; the second most popular for Tennessee, Missouri, and Georgia; and the third most for North Carolina and Florida. *Tenth Census*, 480–483.

12 In 1870, most migrants to McLennan County had come from Alabama, Mississippi, Tennessee, Georgia, and Louisiana. *Ninth Census of the United States, 1870*, vol. 1 (Washington, DC: Government Printing Office, 1872), 372. By 1880, more expansive data added Arkansas, Missouri, Kentucky, and Virginia to this list. *Tenth Census*, 530. Mrs. J. B. Powell, interview by Edward Townsend, July 7, 1938, box 4J132, folder 2, Works Progress Administration Records, 1933–1943, Dolph Briscoe Center for American History, University of Texas at Austin (hereafter cited as WP Records). For representative individual examples of white southerners relocating to Waco to become cotton planters, see Sleeper and Hutchins, *Waco and McLennan County*, 114–116; and "Brown, Henry W." and "Gerald, George Bruce," in *The Handbook of Waco and McLennan County, Texas*, ed. Dayton Kelly (Waco, TX: Texian Press, 1972), 38, 110. Similarly, Patrick G. Williams argued that although the "planter thesis" held for Texas, where antebellum and secessionist leaders regained political power after the war, this was not a simple continuity because they had to contend with different interests as a result of demographic shifts. Williams, *Beyond Redemption*, 5–9.

13 "Chisolm Trail," in *The Handbook of Waco and McLennan County, Texas*, ed. Dayton Kelly (Waco, TX: Texian Press, 1972), 104; *Memorial and Biographical History*, 57; W. R. Poage, *McLennan County before 1980* (Waco, TX: Texian Press, 1981), 59; Sleeper and Hutchins, *Waco and McLennan County*, 62; C. D. Morrison, *General Directory of the City of Waco, for 1878–79* (Waco, TX: Examiner, 1877), 8; "Telegraph—Waco a Cotton Market," *Semi-Weekly Register*, September 29, 1869, box 4J132, folder 1, WP Records.

14 J. W. Riggins, "Big Thing for Texas," *Waco Evening News*, October 10, 1893; promotional pamphlet, "The Texas Cotton Palace," 1894, box 2, folder 8, Texas Cotton Palace Records, accession #792, Texas Collection; J. W. Riggins, "Texas State Cotton Palace," *Waco Evening News*, October 14, 1893.

15 Charles Cutter, *Cutter's Guide to the City of Waco, Texas* (Waco, TX: 1894), 53.

16 Cutter, *Cutter's Guide*, 55; "Texas Cotton Palace," *St. Louis Globe-Democrat*, November 9, 1894; "Social and Current Events," *Artesia*, November 11, 1894; "Where Cotton Reigns," *Marion Daily Star*, December 5, 1894; promotional pamphlet, 1894; "Cowboy Day at Waco," *Galveston Daily News*, December 1, 1894; "The Cotton Palace," *Galveston Daily News*, November 12, 1894.

17 "Negro Day," *Austin Daily Statesman*, November 25, 1894; R. Scott Huffard Jr., *Engines of Redemption: Railroads and the Reconstruction of Capitalism in the New South* (Chapel Hill: University of North Carolina Press, 2019), 101–102; Jane Dailey, Glenda Elizabeth Gilmore, and Bryant Simon, "Introduction," in *Jumpin' Jim Crow: Southern Politics from Civil War to Civil Rights*, ed. Jane Dailey, Glenda Elizabeth Gilmore, and Bryant Simon (Princeton, NJ: Princeton University Press, 2000), 4; Elizabeth Stordeur Pryor, *Colored Travelers: Mobility and the Fight for Citizenship before the Civil War* (Chapel Hill: University of North Carolina Press, 2016), 1–2, 92.

18  "St. Louis Day," *Galveston Daily News*, November 18, 1894; James Morton, "The Cotton Palace," *Daily Tobacco Leaf-Chronicle*, December 1, 1894.

19  Cutter, *Cutter's Guide*, 55; "Pertinent Paragraphs from the Palace," *Artesia*, November 25, 1894; Morton, "Cotton Palace."

20  "Artesian Wells" in *The Handbook of Waco and McLennan County, Texas*, ed. Dayton Kelly (Waco, TX: Texian Press, 1972), 10–11; Cutter, *Cutter's Guide*, 7; *Morrison & Fourmy's General Directory of the City of Waco, 1892–93* (Galveston, TX: Morrison & Fourmy, 1893), 3–4.

21  Cutter, *Cutter's Guide*, 11–15; *Morrison & Fourmy's General Directory of the City of Waco, 1894–95*, 4.

22  "Artesia, The," in *The Handbook of Waco and McLennan County, Texas*, ed. Dayton Kelly (Waco, TX: Texian Press, 1972), 25–26; Cutter, *Cutter's Guide*, 10; "Artesia," *Artesia*, February 19, 1893; William C. Brann, "The Iconoclast Told to Leave Town," in *The Complete Works of Brann: The Iconoclast* (New York: Brann, 1919), 9:204.

23  Brann, "Editorial Etchings," in *Complete Works of Brann*, 7:79; "Social and Current Events," *Artesia*, August 23, 1896; "At the Rink Last Night," *Waco Daily Examiner*, February 28, 1885; "Prince Won the Race," *Waco Evening News*, June 15, 1893; "The Week in Society," *Waco Evening News*, October 28, 1893.

24  Sarah Hallenbeck, *Claiming the Bicycle: Women, Rhetoric, and Technology in Nineteenth-Century America* (Carbondale, IL: Southern Illinois University Press, 2016), 31–32, 132–134; Richard Harmond, "Progress and Flight: An Interpretation of the American Cycle Craze of the 1890s," *Journal of Social History* 5, no. 2 (Winter 1971/1972): 244; "Tea Table Gossip," *Waco Evening News*, May 16, 1893.

25  Brann, "The Bike Bacillus," in *Complete Works of Brann*, 1:253–256; Brann, "Salmagundi," in *Complete Works of Brann*, 11:42; Brann, "Editorial Etchings," *Complete Works of Brann*, 7:80–81; Brann, "Salmagundi," in *Complete Works of Brann*, 5:48.

26  *Davis v. The State*, in *Central Law Journal* 5 (1877): 288; "Untitled," *Waco Daily Examiner*, October 31, 1875, box 4J134, folder 1, WP Records; "Untitled," *Waco Daily Examiner*, January 21, 1876, box 4J135, folder 1, WP Records; Margaret H. Davis, "Harlots and Hymnals: A Historic Confrontation of Vice and Virtue in Waco," *Mid-South Folklore* 4, no. 3 (January 1976): 88; J. T. Upchurch, *Traps for Girls and Those Who Set Them: An Address to Men Only* (Arlington: Purity, 1908), 11, 23; Orville Wilkes, *Diary*, September 30, 1933, Waco, Texas: The Reservation (Vertical File), Texas Collection. The conventional view treats vice as an abstraction rather than deeply embedded in place. See Davis, "Harlots and Hymnals," 92; and Amy S. Balderach, "A Different Kind of Reservation: Waco's Red-Light District Revisited, 1880–1920" (master's thesis, Baylor University, 2005), 4, 35.

27  "Mayor's Court," *Waco Evening News*, May 21, 1892; "An Interesting Decision: In the Police Court Relating to Female Residents of the Reservation," *Waco Evening News*, January 12, 1892; "Police Court," *Waco Evening News*, March 7, 1889. Because social codes conducting prostitutes' behavior were informal, sources are limited to Wacoans recalling the Reservation decades later. See William H. Curry, *A History of Early Waco* (Waco, TX: Texian Press, 1968), 129–130; Davis, "Harlots and Hymnals," 90; and Bob Darden, "Best Legal Whorehouse in Texas," *Dallas Times Herald Westward*, March 27, 1984, Waco, Texas: Prostitution Clippings (Vertical File), Texas Collection.

28  Missouri, Kansas, & Texas Railway Company, *The Opening of the Great Southwest 1870–1945: A Brief History of the Origin and Development of the Missouri Kansas and Texas Rail Way* (M. K. T. Lines, 1945), 2, 6–7; V. V. Masterson, *The Katy Railroad and the Last Frontier* (Norman: University of Oklahoma Press, 1952), 223; *Morrison & Fourmy's General Directory of the City of Waco, 1896–97* (Galveston, TX: Morrison & Fourmy, 1897), 63–66.

29  Cox, *Train Crash at Crush*, 39–48; Frank Barnes, "Train Wreck," *True West*, box 9, folder 5, Thomas E. Turner, Sr. Papers, accession #2200, Texas Collection; Huffard, *Engines of Redemption*, 2, 234–236, 138–139; Scott Reynolds Nelson, *Iron Confederacies: Southern Railways, Klan Violence, and Reconstruction* (Chapel Hill: University of North Carolina Press, 2005), 6–8; Schivelbusch, *Railway Journey*, 129–131. On railroads and modernity, see Leo Marx, *The Machine in the Garden: Technology and the Pastoral Ideal in America* (New York: Oxford University Press, 2000).

30 Schivelbusch, *Railway Journey*, 60–64.

31 "Head-End Collision," *Dallas Morning News*, August 5, 1896; "The Katy's Grand Scientific Show of a Collision"; "Scene of the Collision."

32 "The Collision at Crush," *Houston Post*, September 16, 1896.

33 "They Are All Ready."

34 "Railroad Matters," *Dallas Morning News*, September 11, 1896; "Railroad Matters," *Dallas Morning News*, September 6, 1896; "Is Over at Last"; "Railroad Matters," *Dallas Morning News*, September 12, 1896; Barnes, "Train Wreck," WP Records, 16.

35 "Home Notes and Personals," *Dallas Morning News*, August 14, 1896; "The Crush Collision," *Houston Post*, September 17, 1896; "Is Over at Last."

36 "The Katy Collision Was Entirely Too Realistic—Nine People Were Injured by It," *Austin Daily Statesman*, September 16, 1896; "Collision at Crush"; "Is Over at Last"; "Mrs. Deane on the Crush Collision," *Dallas Morning News*, October 1, 1896.

37 "Stories of Some Witnesses," *Dallas Morning News*, September 17, 1896; Letter, Maggie Dunn to W. H. Clift, September 20, 1896, box 246, folder 20, Crush Collision Collection, accession #1253, Texas Collection.

38 "May Be Another Victim," *Dallas Morning News*, September 17, 1896; "Collision at Crush"; "Katy Collision Was Entirely Too Realistic"; George W. Walling, "Accurate Estimates," *Austin Daily Statesman*, September 20, 1896.

39 "Railroad Matters," *Dallas Morning News*, August 16, 1896; "Deane, Jervis C.," in *The Handbook of Waco and McLennan County, Texas*, ed. Dayton Kelly (Waco, TX: Texian Press, 1972), 84; *Memorial and Biographical History*, 553.

40 Edward A. Berlin, *King of Ragtime: Scott Joplin and His Era* (New York: Oxford University Press, 1994), 28; Rudi Blesh, "Scott Joplin: Black-American Classicist," in *The Complete Works of Scott Joplin*, ed. Vera Brodsky Lawrence (New York: New York Public Library, 1981), 1:xiii–xviii. For criticism of the ending of *Great Crush Collision March*, see Berlin, *King of Ragtime*.

41 "Social and Current Events," *Artesia*, October 4, 1896.

42 Brann, "Salmagundi," in *Complete Works of Brann*, 6:238–239. The ways in which local photographer Fred Gildersleeve portrayed the lynching of Jesse Washington in progress suggests that it too should be understood as a thoroughly modern form of violence marked by the same fascination with speed. Lynching, which white southerners constantly defended as a form of "swift justice," belongs in this conceptual framework of speed grounded in wartime experiences. This adds to a growing literature on lynching as a quintessential feature of modernity rather than southern backwardness. See Grace Elizabeth Hale, *Making Whiteness: The Culture of Segregation in the South, 1890–1940* (New York: Random House, 1998); Jacqueline Goldsby, *A Spectacular Secret: Lynching in American Life and Literature* (Chicago: University of Chicago Press, 2006); and Amy Louise Wood, *Lynching and Spectacle: Witnessing Racial Violence in America, 1890–1940* (Chapel Hill: University of North Carolina Press, 2009). In this light, it may be no coincidence that spectacle lynchings and train crashes crested at the same time. See Huffard, *Engines of Redemption*, 138.

# Grant Park, Atlanta

## An Old South Landscape for a New South City

**A**S CLEMENT A. EVANS, the Confederate general turned Methodist minister, mounted the makeshift pulpit and surveyed his surroundings on April 27, 1890, Atlanta's Grant Park appeared more like a military camp than a public pleasure ground. Rows of white tents were erected on the greensward and hundreds of aged veterans milled about them, or huddled over campfires, as they waited for the sermon that would bring the weekend-long Confederate reunion to a close. Evans began his address with an appeal to the bond that the twinned hardships of the Civil War and Reconstruction had forged between him and his audience: "We were comrades in camp, in march, in battle; comrades through all that we have suffered since; comrades today in our common faith, and I trust we shall be comrades forever." As he enchanted his audience with promises of a prosperous future, Evans urged his listeners to maintain their "old-time integrity, simplicity, chivalry and Faith." Though "the war did not end just as we expected," he explained, "the God of battles has been with us and He is turning upon us a present wealth of blessing in peace that shall fulfil our most patriotic hope." It was through the combination of an established white southern identity and material progress that the South would achieve a cultural victory in place of the military victory that had eluded it twenty-five years prior.[1]

Evans married a glorified past with a utopian future, echoing a central theme of the New South movement. The drive to modernize the region's economy that emerged in the final decades of the nineteenth century relied heavily on nostalgia for a fictive Old South peopled by honorable whites and so-called "contented" Black slaves. As New South boosters championed a model of industrialization and urbanization that mirrored that of the North, they needed to reassure their fellow white southerners that embracing modernity did not require forsaking their cultural identity. They did so by drawing upon the mythology of the Lost Cause, the re-

*by* Steve Gallo

Unidentified visitors at Lake Abana in Grant Park, Atlanta, Georgia, 1895. Photograph from Atlanta History Photograph Collection.

visionist narrative of the Civil War that eased the sting of defeat by romanticizing antebellum society, lionizing the Confederate dead, and valorizing the South's decision to go to war by erasing slavery as the central motivating factor. Combining their message of progress with this emergent civic religion allowed advocates to frame the New South not as a rebuke of the past, but as its validation. This is not to say that such promises were merely empty rhetoric. Boosters, too, sincerely believed that certain features of the Old South needed to be preserved to establish a stable postwar society that maintained a rigid racial hierarchy. At the same time, idyllic depictions of the antebellum South were useful in promoting sectional reconciliation following the Civil War and attracting desperately needed outside investment from the North. Advocates for a New South sought to balance the region's attachment to the past with their drive for change.[2]

Evans's message was not unique in terms of content, but it reveals the important role that space and place played in New South boosters' efforts to reassure the white public that the social structures of the Old South would remain amid the drastic changes of the postwar period. Established in 1883, Grant Park was deliberately constructed as a space in which the Old and

New Souths converged. The park framed modernity as a means of maintaining antebellum culture rather than a divergence from tradition. Its naturalistic design, characterized by dense stands of native trees and fragrant beds of wildflowers, stood in contrast to the ever-expanding city. It was a parcel of Atlanta's prewar landscape preserved from encroachment, and entering the park was like visiting an idealized past. This sense was heightened by physical reminders of the Civil War within the landscape. Rifle pits and breastworks—remnants of the city's wartime defense—were still visible along the park's wooded hills. These design choices invited white visitors to engage with a historical narrative of the Lost Cause. Simultaneously, behavioral regulations, both formal and informal, compelled visitors to maintain the antebellum period's racial and gender hierarchies. Together, these features conflated the region's Confederate history with southern identity by transporting white Atlantans to an imaginary past.

Crucially, the park's effect went beyond simply reaffirming the white public's sense of belonging within a broader southern culture. It instructed visitors on how to reconcile notions of one's self based on nostalgia with the emergent future-oriented society in which they found themselves. Through the unique visual perspective made possible by its geographical location and topographical features, Grant Park functioned as a didactic landscape in which city leaders and designers taught Atlanta's residents how to engage with the past as inhabitants of a New South. In short, the park reinforced a white conception of southern identity and explicitly linked that identity to an agenda of modernization.[3]

The early history of Grant Park helps us better understand the role that cultural memory played in service of the New South movement. More importantly, it reveals how a particular conception of southern identity—one premised upon white patriarchal authority—was promoted by, and codified within, the physical environment. Understanding this process allows us to more critically engage both how the land informs our sense of self and what it means to be a southerner.

**ATLANTA WAS BOOMING** when Grant Park was established in 1883. Thanks to an influx of northern capital, the city had been rebuilt quickly after the combined work of retreating Confederates and advancing Union forces left most of it in smoldering ruins in September 1864. Less than twenty years later, an urban environment that replicated northern forms—complete with new brick buildings and miles of streetcar lines—had risen from the ashes, allowing the city's promoters to frame their hometown as an exemplar of New South success.[4]

Sidney Root, a successful antebellum merchant who spent the war circumventing the Union blockade on behalf of the Confederacy, contributed to this process of modernization as he oversaw the design and improvement of the park from his position as president of the city's newly established park commission. While the scenes of sylvan beauty that he envisioned may, on their surface, seem at odds with Atlanta's sprawl of brick and steel, naturalistic parks were considered staple features of any would-be metropolis of the era. The opening of New York City's Central Park in 1858 not only vaulted its designers, Frederick Law Olmsted and Calvert Vaux, to national fame but initiated a wave of urban park building that swept the country for the remainder of the nineteenth century. Olmsted's firm alone designed, built, or consulted on park projects in at least thirty-five US cities between 1869 and 1900. In keeping with this trend, Root sought to utilize the "fine natural advantages" inherent in the hundred-acre tract in the city's southeastern suburbs by incorporating its rolling hills, thick groves of trees, and natural springs into his design.[5]

Root attempted to maintain the original character of the land, but nonetheless went about "engrafting art upon nature." Between 1883 and 1888, several acres of woodland were cleared to make way for broad expanses of lawn, streams were redirected or bridged, walking paths and carriage roads were cut into the hills, and a large artificial lake was constructed. But Root ensured that these changes were in harmony with the rest of the environment. He had no qualms with diverting a road to spare an especially noble tree and all new planting was done with species native to the region's forests. His goal, he explained, was to "simply aid nature."[6]

The result was a landscape that recalled Atlanta's prewar history, a time in which the burgeoning settlement was, in the words of local doctor and chronicler of Atlanta's history John Stainback Wilson, nothing more than "a city in the woods." When they were adapted to postwar Atlanta, the picturesque design principles that undergirded nineteenth-century parks created a space that corresponded with popular understandings of the city's origin as a frontier settlement carved from the notional "wilderness." Residents could look upon the park's wooded tracts and imagine the same environment that, according to one of Atlanta's nineteenth-century promotional publications, the "axe of the pioneer" worked to clear during the city's founding in the 1830s. White members of the public more closely associated the park's scenery with the past when they juxtaposed it with the rapidly expanding city. To many, it seemed as if a section of the countryside had simply been preserved in the face of urban advance. When *Atlanta Constitution* reporter Wallace P. Reed travelled to the park in 1899, he noted that his fellow visitors were struck by the contrast between the "natural" greenspace and the artificial environment of the rest of modern Atlanta. "Even the most thoughtless," he explained, "had a hazy impression that 'man made the town and God made the country' when they saw the green hills and valleys before them." By reaffirming this distinction between the natural and the human-built, Grant Park promoted the idea that it was possible to travel between two Atlantas: one antebellum and pastoral, the other postbellum and modern. One could see the past in unspoiled nature while the future was made manifest in the built environment. By preserving nature, the park preserved the past.[7]

Root filled the landscape with allusions to Atlanta's history, particularly those that valorized the city's wartime experience. In anticipation of a Union siege during the war, Confederate leaders had forced the local enslaved population to build a series of military fortifications on

Fort Walker in Grant Park, 1895. Photograph by W. H. Parish
Publishing Company, from Atlanta History Photograph Collection.

Atlanta's outskirts. The ruins of the defenses were still visible within the grounds of the park. Root recognized them as a unique attraction and was determined to incorporate them within his improvement plans, especially the remains of a hilltop fort in the park's southeast corner.[8]

He enlisted the help of his close friend Colonel Lemuel P. Grant to help restore the four-gun battery. In addition to his role as the park's benefactor and namesake, Grant had overseen the construction of Atlanta's defenses during the war. He provided the documents needed to ensure that the fort was "restored exactly upon its original plan." Root then wrote to Governor John B. Gordon, himself a former Confederate officer, requesting decommissioned guns from the state arsenal in order to "make the old fort look as near like it did during the war as possible." Gordon responded with a gift of four brass cannons to the park commission in 1887.[9]

Root did not limit himself to historical accuracy, however. He used the restored fort to make Grant Park a sanctified landscape of the Lost Cause. He named it Fort Walker in memory of "the gallant son of Georgia who crimsoned the soil with his life's blood" during the Battle of Atlanta. He then filled it with various war relics that he collected and encouraged members of the public to make their own contributions. The fort soon became a communal reliquary for mementos that celebrated the Confederate defense of the city. Members of the public donated bullets, cannon balls, and unexploded ordnance to "give the place a warlike appearance." One citizen even contributed a human skull that they had unearthed on a nearby battlefield. This collection promoted a retelling of the war that cast the South's motives in the best possible light. By amassing Civil War detritus within a former fort that memorialized a purported martyr, while actively disregarding the Black labor that built the fort, Root framed the conflict as one fought by "confederate heroes who made . . . a fierce defense against fearful odds" rather than a rebellion in the name of preserving slavery. Imbuing physical objects with symbolic meaning and preserving them in a public space provided this narrative with permanency and further reach. As one Atlantan explained, the artifacts were essential for the "new and younger generation" to understand "the stupendous struggles that their fathers endured."[10]

Fort Walker functioned similarly to another space of the Lost Cause located in Grant Park. The *Cyclorama of the Battle of Atlanta*, a massive panoramic painting that showcased a single moment of the city's siege on July 22, 1864, was permanently located in Grant Park in 1892 after completing a national tour. Historian Daniel Judt points out that the ambiguity of the exact moment depicted by the *Cyclorama* allowed for interpretations of a northern or southern victory, depending on the audience. Consequently, Atlantans who saw the painting were encouraged by local newspapers and promotional material to view it through the lens of the Lost Cause. This space, combined with Fort Walker, allowed Grant Park to sustain a white southern identity premised upon a glorified past and perpetuate it among future generations by giving that past physical form.[11]

This spatial manifestation of the Lost Cause increased the mythology's staying power among members of the public. More so than a Confederate monument placed on the town square or a sentimental novel set on an antebellum plantation, Grant Park immersed white Atlantans in a bucolic southern past. Not only did these visitors see the past in the park's idyllic scenery and hear it in the songs of birds that replaced the din of the city, but they *lived* the past while within the grounds. Confederate reunions and Memorial Day celebrations, like the one that brought Evans to Atlanta in 1890, were hosted by veterans' organizations in the park throughout the final decades of the nineteenth century. Audiences that included veterans and the wider public listened as orators drew upon the park's history to solidify a white southern identity defined by Confederate heroism. Governor Gordon, for example, used the scenery to emphasize the bravery and sacrifice of Atlanta's defenders during a reunion of Confederate veterans in 1887. "There is not a square yard . . . on these hills," he told the former soldiers, "that is not rich in the blood of your comrades." Gesturing to specific locations throughout the park, he relied on the greenspace to bring his story to life: "Here was planted the artillery. There stood the infantry in solid lines. There charged the cavalry; and all around us the advancing and retreating federals and confederates left monuments in the bodies of their dead." By grounding his narrative of the war in the landscape, Gordon transformed abstract themes of heroism and sacrifice into a space sanctified by fallen martyrs.[12]

Veterans frequently visited the fort during their reunions for a chance to interact with Root's war relics. In doing so, they recalled their wartime experiences according to the Lost Cause narrative. Several former soldiers at the fort in 1898 were overcome with nostalgia as they looked over the scenery and recounted how "a gallant comrade had fallen near this spot; how another had gallantly defended the colors of his company, or a third had been made captive." By facilitating such romanticized retellings of the war, the park not only maintained Confederate memory but affirmed it as a central component of modern southern identity.[13]

**THE DEFEAT OF THE CONFEDERACY** and the abolition of slavery generated extreme anxiety among white southerners regarding the roles of women and African Americans in postwar society. Both the Civil War and Reconstruction had drastically altered antebellum gender relations by forcing women to provide for their families in the absence of their husbands while abolition disrupted formally institutionalized white supremacy. These shifts were compounded by the rapid rise of southern cities, as urban life presented white women and African Americans with unprecedented opportunity for economic self-determination, personal mobility, and community development. One had only to look at the bustling commercial establishments on Decatur Street that catered to Black clientele or the factories that increasingly employed young white women to see that the social conventions structuring life in antebellum Atlanta had been drastically altered. Consequently, civic leaders and New South proponents sought to reestablish the antebellum hierarchies of race and gender that they equated with a stable society in order to impose order upon chaotic change. Grant Park aided in this effort in Atlanta by providing a controlled environment that limited the impact of shifting gender dynamics and facilitated social interaction according to antebellum norms. Like all nineteenth-century urban parks, it was governed by rules, both explicit and implicit, that were intended to conform visitors to middle-class standards of behavior. Additional de facto regulations, however, ensured that activity within Grant Park mirrored the social hierarchies of the Old South.[14]

Grant Park was a public space in which white women could congregate free from male chaperones and Black Atlantans could enter on their own accord, realities that were unimaginable in the antebellum South. But Grant Park was also one arena, among many, in which Atlanta's white middle-class men and women worked together to recreate the social conditions of the past. Much in the way that historian Karen L. Cox describes white women's central role in disseminating the Lost Cause through public organizations, the behavior promoted by Grant Park represented an "interplay of traditional definitions of womanhood with the new expanded public role of southern white women." The park was part of what historian Georgina Hickey refers to as a "network of female spaces" through which middle- and upper-class white women created an accepted public presence for themselves while reinforcing fundamental tenets of the archetypal southern lady: moral purity, innocence, beneficence, and need for male protection—all values that stemmed from antebellum plantation life and, therefore, rested on a foundation of white supremacy.[15]

The all-male park commission advertised Grant Park as a "safe and delightful place of resort for ladies and children unattended by an escort." This statement acknowledged women's increased autonomy but also assumed their persistent vulnerability in the public sphere. As feminist geographer Leslie Kern explains, building public spaces upon the perceived threat that the city poses to female residents "serves to direct women's fear outwards" and reinforces their reliance on patriarchal institutions for security. In Atlanta, as in the cities throughout the New South, the two primary threats white women faced were understood to be the moral decay that resulted from estrangement from the home and the sexual aggression believed to have proliferated in the wake of Black autonomy. Grant Park purported to insulate female visitors from both. The park commission instituted explicit regulations to make visitors conform to bourgeois conceptions of respectability and make the park, in the words of one promoter, a "safe, free and pleasant resort" by prohibiting profanity, "impure conduct," and alcohol consumption. Shielded from the perceived indecency found throughout the rest of the city, white women could remain secure in their roles as the conduits of the conservative values associated with the Old South.[16]

Activities that took place within the park reinforced antebellum gender roles as well. Picnics, a primary means through which Atlanta's middle-class white women interacted with Grant Park, reinforced domesticity as central to southern womanhood. They varied in size, ranging from small gatherings of friends to dinners for hundreds of children put on by Sunday school-teachers. According to the local press, hosting an outing for a visiting guest allowed young women to exhibit the "social graces and the arts of life" characteristic of southern gentility, for example, while teachers could fulfill their matronly duties by making "lemonade by the gallon for her crowd of little ones." While the teachers' active labor was a departure from the ideal of the antebellum southern lady, who was spared the drudgery of household chores by the oppressions of slavery, it was rendered acceptable by the continued reliance on Black labor. As 92 percent of Atlanta's domestic workers were Black women in 1890, it was common to see them in the park while employed by white families as nurses or caretakers. Similarly, Black women were the only demographic considered suitable to staff the ladies' restroom in the park. When Jacob Haas, Root's successor as president of the park commission, was accused of priv-ileging Black applicants over white ones for the job, he dismissed the claim as ridiculous. "No white woman has ever applied for the position of matron at the public comfort building," he explained, as "it is a servant's place." Unable to reverse the results of emancipation, Atlanta's New South leaders used Grant Park to obscure the reality of Black freedom by rendering the visibility of African Americans within the grounds contingent upon formal subordination. In doing so, they simultaneously reassured white women that the racial hierarchy on which their cultural identity rested would remain in place despite the unfamiliarity of modern urban living.[17]

The park similarly reassured Atlanta's white men of their place in southern society by providing a space in which they could reaffirm their role as head of the family. Numerous articles published in the *Constitution* throughout the 1880s and 1890s pitched outings to Grant Park as a means of preserving a father's relationship with his family even as the demands of urban life increasingly encouraged individuality and socializing outside of the home. "Such days are good things for a man with a family," one explained, "a family picnic is better to the domesticated man than a

An outing at Grant Park, 1908. Photograph from Georgia Archives, Vanishing Georgia Collection.

hundred picnics where other families mix up and spoil things." While modern Atlanta presented men with an abundance of ways to spend their work and leisure hours away from their wives and children, city leaders used Grant Park to reinforce the assumption that their proper place was at the head of their households. In this way, the park served to reassure white men that their primary roles as patriarchs could be sustained in the New South. While the contours of their daily lives may have changed, the fundamental structure of the white family unit remained intact.[18]

Recreating the antebellum gender roles of white women and men required strict adherence to the racial hierarchy of the Old South. While their professional responsibilities formally relegated African American women to positions of subordination within the park, those responsibilities did nothing to restrict the activities of other Black Atlantans who might enter the space as visitors. Accordingly, the space was governed by implicit rules that erased Black agency. Neither the deed that transferred the property to the city nor local laws barred African Americans from entering the park, but there was a clear expectation that those who did would show deference to white visitors. As Reed explained in his 1899 article, "Few negroes go to the park," while those who did belonged to the "better class of their race." He believed that "roughs," or the Black Atlantans that openly challenged white authority, avoided places "where they are certain to meet great numbers of our best people." The repercussions of not adhering to these social expectations were severe. Bob Hunter, for example, met violence when he attended a baseball game in the park in 1890. After confronting a group of white youths who had pelted him with dirt clods, he was chased into the woods and beaten. The boys fractured his skull before the assault was broken up and Hunter was turned over to the police. The expectation of docility toward white visitors, backed up by the threat of violence, resulted in a space governed by an unambiguous racial hierarchy. When paired with the respectability formally sanctioned by the park rules, white women experienced a semblance of the social stability said to have existed before the war.[19]

Despite the park's attempts to conform visitors to elite ideas of respectability, white working-class women favored the dancehalls and commercial establishments downtown. Their preference for recreation deemed distasteful by their middle- and upper-class counterparts resulted in heightened scrutiny of their behavior by the city's reformers in the early 1900s as religious leaders publicly decried cheap amusements as gateways to prostitution and police regularly raided saloons that served female patrons. Efforts to deny Black autonomy were equally fruitless. Rather than relegate African Americans to positions of subordination, the park's strict environment pushed them elsewhere. African American neighborhoods such as Sweet Auburn flourished, as did Black businesses and social institutions. White rage over the persistence of Black autonomy culminated in an eruption of violence in 1906. On September 22, following weeks of unfounded rumors of Black assaults on white women pushed by the local press, thousands of white Atlantans rampaged through the city's downtown in search of victims, beating or shooting any African American they came across while destroying Black-owned businesses. The mob specifically targeted spaces where Black and white Atlantans mixed, such as the city's crowded streetcars and the two entertainment districts along Decatur and Peters Streets, making clear that they considered attempts to simulate antebellum social conditions in venues such as Grant Park to be insufficient. At least twenty-five people were killed and, in an expression of disdain for what they perceived as the New South's excessive racial accommodation, the mob piled many of the bodies at the feet of a memorial to Henry Grady, the movement's most famous spokesman.[20]

**THE EFFORTS OF ATLANTA'S LEADERS** to use Grant Park to hold members of the public to antebellum social conventions generated mixed results, but the space nonetheless helped white Atlantans reconcile their cultural connection to the past with their dedication to New South progress. Maude Annulet Andrews, a columnist for the *Constitution*, tapped into this process when she rode a streetcar to the park in 1888. As she left the city and entered the rural suburbs, she sensed that she was travelling back in time. The car's steam-powered engine struck her as "an unsuitable mode of transportation" once it left the urban environment and entered "God's great hills and valleys." Yet it was this same modern technology that rendered the landscape of the past accessible: the products of New South progress ferried visitors to the Old. At the same time, these technologies required them to be transient. The park's distance from the

Avenue within Grant Park, 1890. Photograph by Art Publishing Company, from Atlanta History Photograph Collection.

city meant the public could access the space only temporarily before having to catch another trolley home, reflecting the New South's relationship with the past. The Old South was to be remembered, revered, and revisited, but not inhabited permanently.[21]

Andrews's nostalgia grew stronger once she entered the park's naturalistic scenery. As she walked along meandering paths through the woods, she turned over leaves in search of fairy umbrella frog stools and ink balls, plants which she described as "magical treasures known to my childhood." But as she reached Fort Walker, the highest point in the park, her perspective changed. From here she conceptualized the city—the clearest manifestation of New South progress—not simply as existing side by side with the Old South, but as a direct outgrowth of its legacy.[22]

Standing on the heights of the fort, Andrews looked below at the "valley of blood which hath ever been the path to great earthly things," before shifting her gaze to the city that appeared as a "phoenix rising from the ashes." Viewed amid such reminders of the past, Atlanta's skyline embodied the victory that the Confederacy had failed to deliver. It was, in Andrews's words, a "world of prosperous peace . . . whose sons and daughters [had] thrown off the mantle of despairing idleness and turned their strong hands to the making of a diadem that will crown their mother the ruling queen of all America." This visual perspective positioned the material prosperity promised by New South boosters as the region's path to redemption. Industrialization and urbanization would succeed where the attempt to establish an autonomous Confederate nation had failed.[23]

While Andrews found hope in the vision of Atlanta's metropolitan future that she glimpsed from the park, she also took comfort in the elements of the past that surrounded it. "Still, there is yet . . . some reminder of the days that have been," she explained. In the valleys to the east, she saw fields of cotton, outstretched like sheets of snow, with overflowing bolls seemingly bent low under the weight of the "past anguish and bloodshed caused by their wealth." Amid the crops, she could make out Black workers tending to the harvest, their labor still tethered for many white southerners to the symbols of bygone antebellum prosperity. Andrews interpreted this sight as evidence that key elements of the old order had endured despite the radical changes wrought by the Civil War. She was reassured by the thought that the Black laborer she stood above remained the "same . . . now as thirty years ago—black, faithful, still a slave in his heart as he picks the white cotton for the white man." The same perspective that positioned the New South movement as the means of elevating Atlanta to its rightful place among the great cities of the United States also assured the city's white citizens that the social structure of the Old South would be maintained. It told them that the abolition of slavery did not mean racial equality. The end of the war may have brought drastic changes to southern society—and modernization promised even more—but New South advocates insisted that central features of the past would remain in place. Grant Park pushed white Atlantans like Andrews to conceptualize this continuity.[24]

Promoting the idea of social continuity through the built environment also ensured that the inequities of the antebellum era persisted into the present. The forms of white supremacy that Andrews propounded from the heights of Fort Walker, for example, not only comforted white Atlantans such as herself, but subjected Black southerners to generations of violence, dispossession, and prejudicial treatment.

By replicating romanticized conditions of antebellum society, Grant Park promoted one conception of southern identity as authentic. Southerners, according to this telling, were those who carved civilization from the wilderness. Southerners were men who fought for a noble cause and sacrificed heroically on its behalf. Southerners were genteel women who maintained their families despite hardship. Southerners were white. New South boosters attempted to render that identity immutable by integrating it into the land itself. In doing so, they set the terms for a new battle that has been, and continues to be, waged across the public spaces of the South. Like Lost Cause iconography, the public parks built across the region during the final decades of the nineteenth century generally privileged white claims to a true southern identity above all others and advanced those claims far into the twentieth century. One needs only to observe the continued efforts of southern activists and lawmakers to remove Confederate monuments from public grounds—and the claims of their defenders that doing so constitutes an assault on southern culture—to understand both the lasting impact of this project as well as the contested nature of its central premise. Despite the efforts of New South leaders to build a society based on their preferred historical memory, the question of how southerners should remember the Civil War and the era that preceded it was far from settled. ❺

1    "Veterans' Lovefeast," *Atlanta Constitution*, April 28, 1890.

2    Historians have long noted the central role that nostalgia for an idealized Old South played in generating support for the New South project. See C. Vann Woodward, *Origins of the New South, 1877–1913* (Baton Rouge: Louisiana State University Press, 1951); Paul M. Gaston, *The New South Creed: A Study in Southern Mythmaking* (Baton Rouge: Louisiana State University Press, 1976); David W. Blight, *Race and Reunion: The Civil War in American Memory* (Cambridge, MA: Harvard University Press, 2001); David Goldfield, *Still Fighting the Civil War: The American South and Southern History* (Baton Rouge: Louisiana State University Press, 2002); James C. Cobb, *Away Down South: A History of Southern Identity* (New York: Oxford University Press, 2005); and Caroline E. Janney, *Remembering the Civil War: Reunion and the Limits of Reconciliation* (Chapel Hill: University of North Carolina Press, 2013).

3    I am building off of the work of Nate Gabriel and applying it to a New South context. Gabriel has shown that the social behavior and visual perspective generated by Philadelphia's Fairmount Park provided a means of conditioning the public into urban subjects. Grant Park served a similar function, but in service of creating subjects suitable to the New South. Nate Gabriel, "The Work that Parks Do: Towards an Urban Environmentality," *Social & Cultural Geography* 12, no. 2 (March 2011): 123–141.

4    William A. Link, *Atlanta, Cradle of the New South: Race and Remembering in the Civil War's Aftermath* (Chapel Hill: University of North Carolina Press, 2013), 55–56; Reiko Hillyer, *Designing Dixie: Tourism, Memory, and Urban Space in the New South* (Charlottesville: University of Virginia Press, 2015), 135; Don H. Doyle, *New Men, New Cities, New South: Atlanta, Nashville, Charleston, Mobile, 1860–1910* (Chapel Hill: University of North Carolina Press, 1990), 34–37.

5    "At the Park," *Atlanta Constitution*, September 26, 1884; "Random Talks," *Sunny South*, August 18, 1883; "The Beautiful Park," *Atlanta Constitution*, April 11, 1886. For more on the importance of naturalistic parks to the nineteenth-century urban landscape, see David Schuyler, *The New Urban Landscape: The Redefinition of City Form in Nineteenth-Century America* (Baltimore, MD: Johns Hopkins University Press, 1986); Galen Cranz, *The Politics of Park Design: A History of Urban Parks in America* (Cambridge, MA: MIT Press, 1982); and Roy Rosenzweig and Elizabeth Blackmar, *The Park and the People: A History of Central Park* (Ithaca, NY: Cornell University Press, 1992). Data related to Olmsted's work on American parks between 1869 and 1900 found in Lucy Lawliss, Caroline Loughlin, and Lauren Meier, eds., *The Master List of Design Projects of the Olmsted Firm, 1857–1979*, 2nd ed. (Washington, DC: National Association for Olmsted Parks, 2008), 39–81.

6    Gail Anne D'Avino, "Atlanta Municipal Parks, 1882–1917: Urban Boosterism, Urban Reform in a New South City" (PhD diss., Emory University, 1988), 51, 57; John Stainback Wilson, *Atlanta As It Is: Being a Brief Sketch of Its Early Settlers, Growth, Society, Health, Morals, Publications, Churches, Associations, Educational Institutions, Prominent Officials, Principal Business Enterprises, Public Buildings, Etc., Etc.* (New York: Little, Rennie, 1871), 6; "The Park," *Atlanta Constitution*, April 19, 1882; "Random Talks"; "The Beautiful Park"; "At the Park"; "Sunday Melange," *Augusta Chronicle*, May 10, 1885.

7    Wilson, *Atlanta As It Is*, 6; "Wallace P. Reed Writes of the Value and Picturesqueness of Grant Park," *Atlanta Constitution*, July 16, 1899. As Reiko Hillyer explains, Atlanta's relatively short antebellum history laid the foundation for a frontier narrative that became central to not only postwar civic identity but to New South boosterism. Hillyer, *Designing Dixie*, 138–141.

8    Link, *Cradle of the New South*, 23.

9    "Grant Park," *Atlanta Constitution*, July 19, 1885.

10  "Sixth Annual Report," *Atlanta Constitution*, January 7, 1889; "Letters from the People," *Atlanta Constitution*, January 10, 1889; "Atlanta's Monuments to Confederate Dead," *Atlanta Constitution*, July 23, 1898; "Cannon Balls," *Atlanta Constitution*, July 12, 1887. I am applying Kenneth E. Foote's definition of a sanctified landscape — "a site set apart from its surrounding and dedicated to the memory of an event, person, or group" — to the Lost Cause, specifically. Kenneth E. Foote, *Shadowed Ground: America's Landscapes of Violence and Tragedy*, rev. ed. (Austin: University of Texas Press, 2003), 8.

11  Daniel Judt, "Cyclorama: An Atlanta Monument," *Southern Cultures* 23, no. 2 (Summer 2017): 30–32.

12  "A Grand Reunion," *Atlanta Constitution*, July 23, 1887.

13  "A Grand Reunion"; "Some Flashlights on Veterans Caught in War and in Peace," *Atlanta Constitution*, July 21, 1898.

14  Georgina Hickey, *Hope and Danger in the New South City: Working-Class Women and Urban Development in Atlanta, 1890–1940* (Athens: University of Georgia Press, 2003), 3–4, 27; Marjorie Spruill Wheeler, *New Women of the New South: The Leaders of the Woman Suffrage Movement in the Southern States* (New York: Oxford University Press, 1993), 9–10; Gregory Mixon, *The Atlanta Riot: Race, Class, and Violence in a New South City* (Gainesville: University Press of Florida, 2005), 4, 12–14, 38; Doyle, *New Men, New Cities*, 261. For more on the ways in which nineteenth-century urban parks functioned as a means of social control, see Roy Rosenzweig, *Eight Hours for What We Will: Workers and Leisure in an Industrial City, 1870–1920*, Interdisciplinary Perspectives on Modern History (New York: Cambridge University Press, 1983); Rosenzweig and Blackmar, *The Park and the People*; Stephen A. Germic, *American Green: Class, Crisis, and the Deployment of Nature in Central Park, Yosemite, and Yellowstone* (Lanham, MD: Lexington Books, 2001); Catherine McNeur, *Taming Manhattan: Environmental Battles in the Antebellum City* (Cambridge, MA: Harvard University Press, 2014), 175–223; and Alvaro Sevilla-Buitrago, "Central Park against the Streets: The Enclosure of Public Space Cultures in Mid-Nineteenth Century New York," *Social & Cultural Geography* 15, no. 2 (December 2014): 151–171.

15  Karen L. Cox, *Dixie's Daughters: The United Daughters of the Confederacy and the Preservation of Confederate Culture*, New Perspectives on the History of the South (Gainesville: University Press of Florida, 2003), 10; Hickey, *Hope and Danger*, 2. For more on the cultural significance of the "southern lady," see Drew Gilpin Faust, *Mothers of Invention: Women of the Slaveholding South in the American Civil War*, Fred W. Morrison Series in Southern Studies (Chapel Hill: University of North Carolina Press, 1996); Catherine Clinton, "Women in the Land of Cotton," in *Myth and Southern History*, ed. Patrick Gerster and Nicholas Cords (Urbana: University of Illinois Press, 1989), 1:107–119; Nina Baym, "The Myth of the Myth of Southern Womanhood," in *Feminism and American Literary History: Essays* (New Brunswick, NJ: Rutgers University Press, 1992), 183–196; and LeeAnn Whites, *The Civil War as a Crisis in Gender: Augusta, Georgia, 1860–1890* (Athens: University of Georgia Press, 1995).

16  Park Commission quote from D'Avino, *Atlanta Municipal Parks*, 57; Leslie Kern, *Feminist City: Claiming Space in a Man-made World* (London: Verso, 2020), 147; Wheeler, *New Women of the New South*, 7; Hickey, *Hope and Danger*, 27; Mixon, *Atlanta Riot*, 4; "The Beautiful Park."

17  Baym, "The Myth of the Myth," 193; "The Society World," *Atlanta Constitution*, April 14, 1888; "Thousands at the Park," *Atlanta Constitution*, May 30, 1897; Howard N. Rabinowitz, *Race Relations in the Urban South, 1865–1890* (New York: Oxford University Press, 1978), 65; *Atlanta Constitution*, October 5, 1899.

18  "The First Day in the Park," *Atlanta Constitution*, April 23, 1893.

19  D'Avino, *Atlanta Municipal Parks*, 56–57; "Wallace P. Reed"; "A Negro with a Pistol," *Atlanta Constitution*, May 24, 1890.

20  Hickey, *Hope and Danger*, 54–58, 73; Mixon, *Atlanta Riot*, 11–14, 85–100.

21  "Pastoral Scenes," *Atlanta Constitution*, November 11, 1888.

22  "Pastoral Scenes."

23  "Pastoral Scenes."

24  "Pastoral Scenes."

Carrie Mae Weems, **Sorrow's Bed**, 2003. Iris print, 20 × 20 in. Photograph from the artist and Jack Shainman Gallery, New York. © Carrie Mae Weems.

# Something That Must Be Faced

## Carrie Mae Weems and the Architecture of Colonization in the *Louisiana Project*

**I**N HER SERIES *(Untitled) Kitchen Table* (1990), photographer Carrie Mae Weems explores and questions perceived notions of racial and racially gendered identity, using the familiar, everyday experience of a woman seated at a domestic kitchen table. Alternating between images of herself alone and with a male lover, child, or with other women, she figures the kitchen table as an architectural space within which to present ideas about tradition, family, monogamy, and relationships. The beautiful, clear-eyed, and complex images in this series established Weems as a photographer politically engaged in critiques of how power is expressed in social space. Yet, Weems has received little attention, to date, for how her photographs of architecture—including antebellum plantation houses (the *Louisiana Project*, 2003), classical buildings in Rome (*Roaming*, 2006), and dwelling structures in western Africa (*Africa*, 1993)—comment on racial subjectivity. In the *Louisiana Project*, Weems highlights the potential of buildings and landscapes to engage discourses of power, identity, gender, and race. By emphasizing architectural space, Weems's black-and-white photographs in the *Louisiana Project* reveal how architectural and preservation practices emerge from and, in turn, influence cultural beliefs about identity and race.

*by* Claire Raymond *and* Jacqueline Taylor

Weems undertook the *Louisiana Project* in response to an invitation from Tulane University's Newcomb Art Gallery and New Orleans officials to contribute to the city's bicentennial commemoration of the Louisiana Purchase (1803), which marked a critical moment in North American history. It added well over eight hundred thousand square miles of territory to the United States, while also assuring an aggressive push westward that resulted in the deaths of thousands of Native Americans, the near destruction of many aspects of Indigenous life and culture, and effectively extended the practice of enslavement into new territories. For her contribution to the bicentennial, Weems identified architecture as a critical component in shaping African American cultural identity. In her photographs, she used her own figure to bear witness, standing as a vivid, living symbol for the cultural history of colonization and its continuing impact on Black communities. Clothed in period costume, Weems's figure is spectral and suggests the force of cultural haunting. For Weems, history inheres in architectural forms and in the bodies of living human beings who descend from and inherit the as yet unresolved terms of settler colonialism. The *Louisiana Project* juxtaposes antebellum buildings that have been kept pristine into the twenty-first century with industrial spaces—landscapes scarred by rusting gas tanks, railroads, and mass-produced housing for impoverished and African American residents. Her photographs transform our way of seeing, challenging conventions of architectural photography by inserting her own body as witness figure. She observes these architectures from the implied perspective of a ghost, her gaze a critique of longstanding structures of racism.

---

Dressed in nineteenth-century calico garb, Weems presents herself in *A Distant View* seated in the lengthy shadow of a large tree, the leafy canopy of which frames a view of an antebellum mansion. The photograph's formal composition, with its soft focus and shadowy framing, emphasizes the stark white forms of an elegant building set against a lush landscape and bright sky. In view is the René Beauregard House, so named for its later owner—a high court judge and son of prominent Confederate army officer Pierre Gustave Tourant Beauregard. Situated on the banks of the Mississippi River two miles south of New Orleans, the house was originally designed in the French Colonial style around 1832 and remodeled by architect James Gallier Sr. in the late 1950s.[1]

The structure included elaborate, decorative trappings of classical Greek architecture with eight double-height Doric columns forming front and rear galleries that lent expanded space and height to the body of the building. There were four symmetrically placed double-height French windows with fine details, such as pedimented dormers and a decorative entablature connecting columns to a steeply pitched roof. This classical architectural vocabulary served to advertise what the patrons considered their rightful place in the crucible of civilization:

ancient Greece. The popular Greek Revival style, combined with the choice of architect (Gallier went on to design the much-admired New Orleans City Hall), symbolized the taste, sophistication, and social status to which Louisiana's antebellum elite aspired. To sustain this ambition, large numbers of enslaved people toiled in households and distant fields. These individuals lived in separate quarters or in the lofts of outbuildings like kitchens and washhouses. Whether laboring indoors or out, enslaved people remained unseen by white landowners, but as folklorist John Michael Vlach has asserted, "Beyond the white master's residence, back of and beyond the Big House, was a world of work dominated by

Black people. The inhabitants of this world knew it intimately and they gave to it, by thought and deed, their own definition of place."[2]

In a caption, Weems gives one of these unseen, unheard women a voice:

> I was not amongst the gentle crowd of ragged negroes gathered together in the evening to stand under the old oak tree and sing sad spirituals, while the gentleman of the house and his guests reflected with glee, the naturalness of their privilege. No, I was the chambermaid, the whore and the witness.

Employing a timer to create the *Louisiana Project* photos, Weems directs her view toward buildings and landscapes, away from viewers, so that we see her back in every image and, rarely, a trace of her profile. Seldom does Weems turn to face us. In posing as a silent observer engaging with the cultural landscape before her, she characterizes this environment as something that must be faced. This stance implicates the audience. As photographer Deborah Willis notes, Weems's use of her own figure in her photographs doubles the gaze implied in the image: as she witnesses, we are also privy to the relationship of this figure to the buildings and landscapes before which she stands. The witness figure testifies to the presence of enslaved African Americans in those historic antebellum scenes, forcing a consideration of the built environment through her eyes. By positioning her body in this way and wearing nineteenth-century clothing, Weems appears as a ghostly survivor of enslavement.[3]

---

In *Passageway II*, Weems photographs herself framed by the columns of the Beauregard House, looking out to the landscape beyond. She suggests that the viewer reflect on the position of Black bodies in antebellum Louisiana, framed within the architecture yet within sight of a horizon unconstrained by built forms. The figure's back is turned and her body is centered in the structure's heavy-columned frame. The deceptively beautiful neoclassical columns of the Old South impose a heavy weight upon African Americans yearning for the unburdened, liberated horizon. In contrast to the frame's depth and darkness, the plantation beyond it appears vast, a domain of colonized space that holds tragic histories. Weems, the observer, remains steady, her gaze directed determinedly outward, unerring. The photograph suggests a passage through this architecture and a way beyond its oppressive historical constraints to the hopeful possibilities of northern cities where Black people could imagine living as free people.

When Weems photographs herself standing before antebellum mansions around New Orleans, she confronts architecture built with the white supremacist dream of oppressing Blackness — oppressing knowledge of Africa, and African forms, languages, and culture. Constructed as a French port city, and briefly managed by the Spanish monarchy, the city expanded its identity with

the Louisiana Purchase to become increasingly diverse demographically, economically, and culturally. During the early years of settlement, the French established a unique but nevertheless exploitative caste (or *plaçage*) system, legally recognizing the "mistress" relationship between a white man and a woman of African descent. These women and the descendants of their unions were classified as mixed-race, creating a third caste, or group known as *gens de couleur*, or free people of color, who, because of their acknowledged familial relationship to the dominant white class, complicated the racialized landscape, laying claim to privileges and social activities unique to New Orleans, such as annual

Mardi Gras balls. Although free women of color were granted some recognition as the bearers of white French or Spanish settler children, they were never fully accepted into the ruling class nor did they identify with the enslaved people of color. Excluded from the true world of white privilege, and self-segregated from the enslaved community, this mixed-race group of free people of color made its own spaces of relative freedom that were nevertheless separate.[4]

Weems seems to refer to the women of this third caste in a triptych of images, *A Single's Waltz in Time*. Framed within the luxurious interior space of another plantation mansion and once again dressed in calico, Weems dances barefoot with mournful grace. For once, she faces the viewer, then spins around, defiantly commanding the room, and intensifies this gesture of claiming the space by capturing it in the lens of her camera. The parlor was a fraught area in traditional southern society. It bespoke class privilege and was the particular site wherein white women demonstrated their social power over Black bodies.

A ghost figure dances through the parlor at Nottoway Plantation. The mansion was built for the Virginia-born sugar planter John Hampden Randolph, an interloper who installed himself among the wealthiest of New Orleans, intent, after the Louisiana Purchase, on forging a new American identity in the formerly French colonial landscape. In 1857, Randolph engaged Henry Howard, an Irish craftsman who apprenticed with architecture firms in New York and New Orleans to become a leading local architect (and, as such, exemplary of how white labor functioned in the plantation economy). Howard partnered with another immigrant, Albert Diettel, a German mason and engineer, who also worked his way from New York to New Orleans. The two made drawings and plans according to Randolph's specifications, resulting in a massively proportioned Greek-Revival-Italianate design to compete with John Andrews's

neighboring mansion Belle Grove, completed that same year. Randolph's highly ornate double parlor, known as "the ballroom," staged debutante dances and served as the venue for the weddings of his five daughters.[5]

Is Weems's barefoot, dancing form the unacknowledged Black Creole mistress, the "chambermaid, the whore" of *A Distant View*, who now stakes her claim to a place within the house? Here, Weems is suggesting the subtle and not-so-subtle social bondage of the systems of plaçage and enslavement. The "chambermaid, the whore" is specifically she who, by dint of race and class, cannot have social privilege in the public domestic sphere of the parlor. Her exclusion from this social space is made tangible by a structure emphasizing the white supremacist vision of so-called Western cultural superiority. These are architectural spaces of grief where women of African descent inhabit a realm entrapped within the white cultural dream of a life free from toil and care. Wealthy white women do not labor in parlors; they preside. The parlor signifies heavily in southern cultural practices where young white women were celebrated, and introduced to their peers and potential suitors, for example. The parlor is the space of utmost entertainment, where white families showed their wealth and dominion in a space they in fact shared with laboring Black enslaved people. Weems's period garment places her in the realm of the woman of African descent whose body is constrained and unfree in white-dominated architectural spaces. Her witness figure here portrays both the enslaved woman of African descent and the Creole mistress.[6]

The dance, in this triptych, is a mournful declaration of freedom, the freedom of a Black female body to move to its own rhythm and desire, to lay claim to the space of the parlor that is a showpiece of white supremacy. The figure in the mantel painting, its head occluded by the sumptuous chandelier, stands blindly. And though that figure cannot see Weems's dance, Weems nonetheless commandeers the hearth space in the sight line of the camera. The high ceilings and ornate molding convey the building's impassive neoclassical aesthetic in contrast to the dancer's expressive posture.

In further photographs, Weems compares the antebellum architectures pristinely preserved in twenty-first-century New Orleans with constructions from other periods in the city's history. In *In the Abyss*, she faces a housing project built in the late 1930s as a federally funded response to homelessness and unsanitary Depression-era living conditions. These low-rise brick superblocks were initially intended for whites but were opened up to African Americans after passage of the 1964 Civil Rights Act. The hope they signaled for better accommodation dissolved rapidly into the racialized categories of segregation, discrimination, poverty, crime, and neglect, disenfranchising and trapping African Americans once again.[7]

*In the Abyss* depicts Weems as the enigmatic nineteenth-century spectral figure engaging this building head on. Its three-storied brick facade towers above her. Folding chairs, a small BBQ grill, and other material artifacts of a hot and humid quotidian South spill out and clutter the narrow, shared balcony that runs the length of the building. The housing project fills the frame of vision so that we, the audience, see no escape from the abyss. The *Louisiana Project* photographs work by implicit comparison, as Weems shows antebellum mansions and contrasting hardscrabble industrial neighborhoods. *In the Abyss* stands in stark contrast to Weems's photograph of the Beauregard House, which is shown in its totality with sky and lawn and trees softly framing the image, emphasizing the totalizing effect of white supremacy. The housing project, strikingly, is fragmented, cut off and tightly contained by the photograph's frame. Laid bare in the aftermath of Hurricane Katrina, the city's quarters reveal racist social patterns wherein substandard housing in predominantly Black neighborhoods, impacted by decades of redlining, was exceedingly vulnerable to devastation.[8]

In one untitled photograph, Weems looks down the length of a railroad line. In another, she faces a sign painted on the edge of a building that advertises alcoholic beverages, a solution often sought to alleviate the despair and demoralization of those trapped in a cycle of unemployment and few resources. Both images connect to a broader history of segregation, longing, rootlessness, and despondency. The African diaspora created a people in constant motion, as enslaved labor shifted across antebellum plantation landscapes and as people sought freedom and opportunity after (and sometimes during) enslavement. Many people of African descent in the Americas would eventually join northbound trains to more hopeful, yet always uncertain, places, where they were often met with forms of structural racism promulgated beyond the traditional South.

Weems's photographs depict a cultural landscape, dominated by white supremacy, that has denigrated African Americans, excluding visual clues of their positive contributions and reducing them to stereotypes, a situation that shockingly persists even where communities of color predominate. The architectures of white supremacy create ghettoization. When Weems includes herself in images of architecture, she creates tableaux that tell more complete and deeply troubling stories. Putting woman front and center as director of the gaze disrupts long-held and accepted narratives. In a recent interview about her work, Weems acknowledged her drive to be "a critically engaged woman" rather than the "social activist" she is often considered. Consistently using her own female Black body, Weems draws on James Baldwin's stance that the artist's job is to illuminate, insisting on this demystifying gaze from a woman's perspective. In reenvisioning the habitation of architectural spaces that were built to hold hierarchy in place, she subversively reinserts her body as a critical tool to pose the deep question of "who we are as humans" and for Weems the artist,

Carrie Mae Weems, **Untitled (Standing on the Tracks)**, 2003. Gelatin silver print, 20 × 20 in. Photograph from the artist and Jack Shainman Gallery, New York. © Carrie Mae Weems.

Carrie Mae Weems, **Untitled (Woman Facing Industrial Landscape)**, 2003. Gelatin silver print, 20 × 20 in. Photograph from the artist and Jack Shainman Gallery, New York. © Carrie Mae Weems.

this always begins with herself as a moral force up against the dominating power in whatever form it may take, expressed here in the surrounding structures. As architectural critic Sarah Williams Goldhagen argues, "A change in a visual axis, or spatial sequence, or the way solids are massed and volumes composed could ignite very different cognitions." In challenging the hierarchical force of the architectures of white supremacy, Weems opens not only new ways but also new visual spaces for seeing. Through her witnessing gaze, the oppressive history of New Orleans's built environment is revealed and also revitalized as social space ripe for negotiation. She makes a claim on that space as a Black woman artist—a claim that extends through the *Louisiana Project*'s image field to all people of the African diaspora.[9] ⑤

---

NOTES

1  Kevin Risk, "Chalmette Battlefield and Chalmette National Cemetery Cultural Landscape Report," NPS, 1999; "The Rene Beauregard House," Historic Resource Study (Chalmette Unit) NPS, 2004.

2  Catherine Clinton, *The Plantation Mistress: Woman's World in the Old South* (New York: Pantheon, 1982); John Michael Vlach, *Back of the Big House: The Architecture of Plantation Slavery* (Chapel Hill: University of North Carolina Press, 1993), 1–2.

3  Carrie Mae Weems, Susan Cahan, and Pamela R. Metzger, *Carrie Mae Weems: The Louisiana Project* (New Orleans: Newcomb Art Gallery, 2005); Deborah Willis, "Translating Black Power and Beauty: Carrie Mae Weems," *Callaloo* 35, no. 4 (Fall 2012): 993–996.

4  Lisa Ze Winters, *The Mulatta Concubine: Terror, Intimacy, Freedom, and Desire in the Black Transatlantic* (Athens: University of Georgia Press, 2018); Amy R. Sumpter, "Segregation of the Free People of Color and the Construction of Race in Antebellum New Orleans," *Southeastern Geographer* 48, no. 1 (May 2008): 19–37.

5  Robert S. Brantley, *Henry Howard: Louisiana's Architect* (New York: Princeton Architectural Press, 2015).

6  Weems, Caban, and Metzger, *Carrie Mae Weems*; Justin A. Nystrom, *New Orleans after the Civil War: Race, Politics, and a New Birth of Freedom* (Baltimore, MD: Johns Hopkins University Press, 2010).

7  Susan Caban, "Carrie Mae Weems: Reflecting Louisiana," in Carrie Mae Weems, *The Louisiana Project* (New Orleans: Newcomb Art Gallery, Tulane University, 2003); Karen Kingsley and Lake Douglas, Bienville Basin Apartments (Iberville Housing Development), Society of Architectural Historians Archipedia, https://sah-archipedia.org/buildings/LA-02-OR33.

8  Rebecca Solnit, *A Paradise Built in Hell: The Extraordinary Communities that Arise in Disaster* (New York: Penguin, 2010).

9  "Art and Activism: A Conversation with Carrie Mae Weems and Khary Lazarre-White at NeueHouse," The Brotherhood/Sister Sol, July 22, 2020, July 22, 2020, https://brotherhood-sistersol.org/psa-from-carrie-mae-weems/; Sarah Williams Goldhagen, *Welcome to Your World: How the Built Environment Shapes Our Lives* (New York: HarperCollins, 2017), 92.

# The Great Unbuilding

## Land, Labor, and Dispossession in New Orleans and Honduras

**W**HEN THE BODY OF JOSE PONCE ARREOLA—one of three workers killed during the October 12, 2019 collapse of the Hard Rock Hotel in New Orleans—was finally removed from the hotel ruins in August 2020, the press asked his brother, Sergio, what should be built once the rubble was cleared. Sergio said, "A park dedicated to the workers who died." The reporter followed up, "No hotel?" He replied pithily, "No."[1]

For several months after the collapse, the south-facing side of the unfinished Hard Rock Hotel, located just off the famed French Quarter, remained in ruins, like the smashed end of a layer cake. Thirteen stories of twisted metal beams and crumpled concrete floors contrasted with upright yellow cranes bookending the ruins. The noncollapsed side remained incomplete, its lower levels enveloped in dark violet and gold siding, hinting at the triad of Mardi Gras hues: purple, gold, and green.

As the building collapsed, over one hundred construction workers and pedestrians fled to safety. Buckling floors and falling debris ultimately killed three construction workers—Ponce,

*by* Deniz Daser *and* Sarah Fouts

View of the collapsed Hard Rock Hotel construction site, February 2020.
Photograph by Kelly van Dellen, from Alamy Stock Photo.

Anthony Magrette, and Quinnyon Wimberley—and injured dozens. Yet, before the tragedy, workers had documented the hazardous conditions of a structurally flawed building, sharing footage of beams bending at pressure from too much weight on social media. GIS data showed that three city inspectors signed off on the construction site without ever visiting it. As inspectors, developers, and contractors cut corners, investigations in the aftermath exposed jarring depths of neglect, absence of oversight, and an egregious disregard for human life.[2]

Joel Ramirez, one of the injured workers, spoke to the media about the dangerous conditions at the worksite. Soon after blowing the whistle, Ramirez, who had resided in the United States for nearly twenty years, was detained and quickly deported by Immigration and Customs Enforcement (ICE) back to Honduras. Until August 2020, the bodies of Wimberley and Ponce remained trapped in the derelict building.

This is a transnational tale of building: the Hard Rock Hotel's edifice skirting the edge of the touristic French Quarter, partially realized as a multinational corporate project, grounded within centuries of racial capitalism and labor exploitation, and reliant on migrant labor. Outsiders at once lionize New Orleans for its indefatigable merriment and tolerance for gluttony, which Lynnell L. Thomas calls "desire," while simultaneously reproaching the city for its corruption, racial capitalism, and narratives of violence, which Thomas calls "disaster." Locals feel a complex and sometimes unconditional love for this precise messiness that creates the place's joie de vivre. As paradoxes abound, desire becomes commodified, whitewashed, and central to tourism narratives while funds are diverted from the public sector.[3]

Thus, this is also a tale of unbuilding, a great undoing of government in favor of privatization, a chiseling away at public oversight and workers' rights. Deregulation in the name of economic development stretches beyond New Orleans to Honduras, where residents have been displaced because corporations have seized land in a bid to capitalize on an ever-hungry tourism industry.

Extractive policies and efforts to privatize often take place on a global scale, spanning from "banana republics" to rebuilding efforts after Hurricane Katrina. Situating the US South within the circum-Caribbean region and linking places like Honduras (where Ramirez is from) and

Emergency officials on scene at the collapsed Hard Rock Hotel, October 12, 2019. Photograph by Emily Kask, from AFP via Getty Images.

New Orleans (where he settled) reveals the Hard Rock Hotel site's place within far-reaching historical and transnational contexts. Addressing the political economy of redevelopment in the wake of Hurricane Katrina in 2005, George Lipsitz suggests that city officials and private developers used the city's Black culture to promote its tourism industry while displacing the same people who made this rich history possible. Lipsitz shows how racial capitalism—capitalist accumulation made possible through systemic racial subordination and exploitation—is employed through the extractive tourism industry in concert with megaprojects, multinational hotels, and other corporate chains that take precedence over the people, labor, and history that make a place meaningful. New Orleans's history as a central port in the trans-Atlantic slave trade has played a role in centuries of segregation and racial inequity that persist to the current era, as the uneven effects of Katrina's destruction and displacement highlight. Racial capitalism presently unfolds via deregulation and privatization that has occurred since the 1970s, further entrenching inequality in the aftermath of Katrina and beyond. Experiences of exploitation, appropriation, and corruption are reminiscent of similar circumstances in the places migrants leave behind. Examining labor flows between Central America and the US South reveals parallels between extractive practices in these two postdisaster contexts on a global scale.[4]

## The Long Road to the Hard Rock Hotel

The fall of the Hard Rock Hotel begins with the troubled legal history of its developer. The majority owner of the hotel, Mohan Kailas, operated with his team under 1031 Canal Street Developers, one of many LLCs used for his more than one hundred residential and commercial ventures across the city. The LLC hides his own name, one that is tattered by hundreds of thousands of dollars of unpaid inspection fees and questionable political contributions. One of these shady dealings led to the 2013 conviction of Mohan Kailas's son, Praveen, for conspiracy and theft of public funds from the post-Katrina Road Home project, the largely failed government program that funded homeowners to either rebuild or sell their damaged homes. During the sentencing, which sent Praveen to federal prison for thirty days, the judge scolded Mohan, accusing him of letting his son take the fall for him.[5]

Kailas's reach extends to the halls of city government. Investigative reporters for the Lens linked almost $70,000 of campaign donations from Kailas to Mayor Latoya Cantrell along with over $20,000 of donations to former and current city council members. City council votes were essential to grant Kailas the right to begin building the two hundred–foot Hard Rock Hotel building that defied zoning regulations (then capped at seventy-five feet) and Historic District of Landmarks Commission standards, including the right to demolish the building already onsite. To make way for the hotel, Kailas's team bulldozed the historic deco-style Woolworth building where the Congress on Racial Equality led the first New Orleans sit-ins protesting racial segregation on September 9, 1960. No memorial has ever been erected to commemorate the New Orleans sit-in.[6]

In 2018, Kailas unveiled designs for an eighteen-story, 350-room, mixed-use development with the Florida-based Hard Rock International. The Hard Rock Hotel is an expansion of the multinational Hard Rock Café Inc., a global chain that occupies the entertainment center of almost every major city and offers a cookie-cutter corporate experience filled with guitars, hamburgers, and memorabilia. You know the T-shirt. The head of Hard Rock Hotel's development

**The south-facing side of the unfinished Hard Rock Hotel remained in ruins,** like the smashed end of a layer cake.

explained the corporation's aspirations: "As Hard Rock continues to expand globally, our focus will be influential cities with deep musical roots," and described New Orleans as "home to a unique melting pot of cultures." The Hard Rock Hotel brings a corporate homogeneity to a city that is anything but mass-produced. As developers like Kailas build over local histories and foster the arrival of salable cultural spaces, they also use a precarious workforce to carry out this corporate vision in the wake of post-Katrina's urban restructuring.[7]

## Rebuilding in Post-Katrina New Orleans

Workers in post-Katrina New Orleans's construction and hospitality industries come up against wage theft, work injury, and, for undocumented workers, constant insecurity due to possible detainment and deportation. These experiences, however, are far from anomalous. After the levees broke in 2005, the Bush administration immediately suspended federal labor regulations that guaranteed prevailing wages and Occupational Safety and Health Administration protections. Black workers, who make up the bulk of New Orleans's working class, faced flooded homes and massive layoffs. The forced displacement of these workers, coupled with the suspension of federal policies to protect labor, led to their replacement with migrant workers. A new, post-Katrina labor force saw tens of thousands of migrants working under massive deregulation and an increasingly draconian federal immigration machine. Many of the immigrant workers who risked life and limb working in the dangerous sector of cleanup and rebuilding stayed in New Orleans and, like Ramirez, settled in neighborhoods and started families. Well over a decade after Katrina, a robust construction industry and bustling tourism sector have kept these immigrants employed.[8]

Yet, whether in construction or hospitality, low-wage workers experience highly abusive conditions. With average pay well below the living wage, service work in the hotel industry is also characterized by a lack of paid sick days, paid vacation days, benefits, promotions, and the ability to set regular working hours. Exploited workers who build the hotels construct the same walls that lock in the low-wage, overworked staff who prepare etouffees, Sazerac cocktails, and plush accommodations for tourists.

Across the United States, right-to-work laws make it exceedingly difficult to organize unions. New Orleans's hotels employ 11,647 people, or about 5.6 percent of the city's jobs. While

worker-centered organizations like the New Orleans Hospitality Workers Alliance offer some support for low-wage workers, only three hotels—Harrah's, Hilton Riverside, and Loew's—of a staggering 161 are unionized. For the construction industry, subcontracting became common during the deregulation that began in the 1980s. The number of unionized construction workers dropped from 80 percent in 1973 to 14 percent in the early 2010s, even while the number of construction workers doubled. This overall decline in unionization in New Orleans mirrors national trends that began in the 1970s and have continued through the twenty-first century.[9]

Louisiana's big business agendas block a state minimum wage and state-level Department of Labor. Little to no public funding is made available for worker organizations or legal services for low-wage earners. Along with right-to-work laws in the US South, policies that favor capital over labor, such as tax incentive schemes, bring an increased corporate presence with the promise of creating jobs. Politicians and key stakeholders' concerns center on bringing in corporate revenue that attracts outsiders, rather than supporting small, locally-owned business-

View from Canal Street, a common route for passersby, tourists, locals, and Mardi Gras parades, January 20, 2021. Photograph by Fernando López.

es. Heralded for creating 250 jobs, recently retired and beloved Saints NFL quarterback Drew Brees opened eight Champaign, Illinois–based Jimmy John's franchises across the po-boy city.[10]

Yet, these policy decisions are rooted in histories of exploitation and neglect. In the words of Natalie, a labor organizer and lawyer, the systems themselves are "built to keep people poor so that they'll continue to work shitty jobs that they don't get paid for. This is the economy of the South. That has been the economy of the South since England and Spain and everyone colonized it, right?" Natalie helped to run a voluntary Wage Claim Clinic in New Orleans in the mid-2010s helping workers—documented or not—receive back pay, overtime, or a range of other due compensation that falls under the umbrella term of "wage theft." Many of the workers seeking help at the clinic were construction workers, not unlike Magrette, Wimberley, Ponce, and Ramirez. Others were hospitality workers, laboring in hotels, restaurants, bars, and other entertainment venues. For many of the labor lawyers and federal employees volunteering at places like the Wage Claim Clinic, the experience of measuring and acting against disparities is Sisyphean.[11]

The decline of workers' rights paralleled a nationwide increase in undocumented immigration and simultaneous detention and deportation under the Clinton administration in the 1990s. Post-9/11 policy changes under Bush, including the creation of Homeland Security and ICE, ushered in a particularly draconian era of immigration enforcement that took aim at postdisaster worksites. Rhetoric of illegality and deportability become a disciplinary mechanism to produce pliable, exploitable workers. Ramirez's forced removal after speaking out against shoddy workplace conditions reveals a more explicit form of deportation based on retaliation. Under the Trump administration, over twenty immigrant rights activists entered deportation proceedings as punishment for their activism.[12]

Yet, such worker struggles have not meant a dearth of political resistance. After Hurricane Katrina, Black workers, largely shut out of the rebuilding, and immigrants, subject to unsafe working conditions, organized under the larger umbrella of the New Orleans Workers' Center for Racial Justice (NOWCRJ). Though just one actor within a larger patchwork of vibrant social justice organizing, their multiracial solidarity organizing has led to lasting changes in local city governance. The Congress of Day Laborers, a suborganization of NOWCRJ led by undocumented migrants in the city, launched a campaign to stop Ramirez's deportation. While the campaign proved unsuccessful, it united local nonprofits, building trade union members, and undocumented workers. The movement exposed the gravity of deporting Ramirez and illustrated how ICE, acting as an arm of the state weaponized for the business sector, silenced a crucial witness. Today, Ramirez, forced to leave his wife and three kids behind, is living in Honduras after speaking out about the unsafe work conditions of the very building that killed his colleagues.

Like New Orleans, the Honduran state has instituted "open for business" policies and pushed for the expansion of extractive tourism industries that operate at the expense of poor and working-class communities. Just as Hurricane Katrina led to a disaster capitalism complex that included deregulation, extreme privatization, and the dismantling of the public sector, Hurricane Mitch, which devastated Honduras in 1998, led to increased privatization and dispossession of Honduran lands by these tourism industries. The aftermath of the 2009 coup of Manuel Zelaya, whose administration sought to redistribute and better protect land from corporations, further expedited these reforms, ushering in over a decade of austerity and unfettered corporatism. This shift to a highly privatized market-based economy with a significantly weakened public sector has contributed to the instability and displacement that forced people to leave the country in search of opportunity in cities like New Orleans — including construction work on the Hard Rock Hotel.[13]

## Tracing Legacies of Graft, Development, and Displacement to Honduras

Just over fifty miles northeast of Ramirez's current home in the Department of Yoro is Indura Beach and Golf Resort, a high-end hotel and spa that occupies over twenty-six miles of Honduras's Caribbean coast. According to Indura's website, the beach resort's "overall design remains true to the region's history," a reference that unwittingly connects to the banana trade and neocolonial history of United Fruit Company (UFC), now Chiquita Brands. Headquartered in New Orleans for much of the twentieth century, UFC's plantations and offices spread along the same coastal lands where Indura now resides.[14]

Indura is a lavish display of abundance with faux-thatched roofs, eco-adventures, and an 1,800-acre, eighteen-hole golf course; all situated in a region plagued by corruption, violence, poverty, and environmental devastation. Initially sponsored by the Honduran government, private investors, and partial funding from the Inter-American Development Bank, the hotel is now part of the upscale Curio Collection by the multinational Hilton Hotel conglomerate.

On its website, Indura boasts that its wellness spa treatments reflect Honduras's "mélange of cultural influences"—influences built upon the ancestral lands of the Garifuna, Black Indigenous people exiled from Yurumein (now St. Vincent) Island by the British in 1797 and forced to Roatan, a small island off the coast of Honduras. The Garifuna people eventually settled across coastal Central America, establishing their own villages and cultural practices that include traditional dances, foods, and the preservation of their language that showcases their Carib and Arawak roots. Since 2001, the Garifuna language, dance, and music have been protected under UNESCO's Intangible Cultural Heritage of Humanity.[15]

Even though some Garifuna communities were granted territorial rights through the

Protesters march down Canal Street alongside the remains of the Hard Rock Hotel, January 20, 2021. The site became a stop for several marches and public demonstrations for over a year. Photograph by Fernando López.

Honduran constitution to hold communal land titles in perpetuity, a mushrooming tourist industry—empowered by a corrupt government and corporatism—has sought out their beachfront property and slowly chipped away at their land. Since this restructuring, which began in the mid-1990s, Black Indigenous people have struggled against Indura's expansion because, much like the Hard Rock Hotel, Indura's developers thrive on cronyism and deregulation. These local communities have been razed to make way for more hectares of golf courses, bike paths, and palm tree–lined protections for tourists. Along with real estate speculation, the expansion of palm oil plantations and deregulation of gas and oil industries have led to

irreversible environmental devastation of wetlands and mangroves while also engendering violent land grabs that threaten the local Garifuna communities. All this happens with the support of the procorporatist Honduran government.[16]

Groups like OFRANEH (Black Fraternal Organization of Honduras) and COPINH (Council of Popular and Indigenous Organizations of Honduras) have fought against privatization efforts only to be violently targeted by militarized forces and private companies working in tandem with the Honduran state. Notably, Berta Cáceres, a Honduran activist and winner of the illustrious international environmental award the Goldman Prize, was murdered point blank in 2015 for her activism to end the construction of a hydroelectric dam project proposed by the private energy company DESA. David Castillo Mejia, a Honduran ex-military intelligence officer (trained at West Point) and president of DESA, was charged for her murder and awaits trial.[17]

More recently, in early June 2020, Garifuna leader Antonio Bernádez, who fought relentlessly for land rights and whose daughter is an activist in New Orleans, was murdered in what many consider retaliation for his activist work. Just weeks later, five Garifuna leaders were kidnapped on July 19, 2020, and forced at gunpoint from their respective homes into unmarked vehicles. The leaders' whereabouts are still unknown. In New Orleans, those who speak out against labor abuses and unfettered capitalism are subject to deportation. In Honduras, this activism can be fatal.[18]

At Barra Vieja, a local Garifuna village that the Indura expansion has slowly swallowed, thatch-roofed houses made of wood scatter the beachfront property. With a squint, the fencing for the giant Indura hotel complex is visible, ensconced by the dense, pruned foliage that evokes a mutable yet protected divide. In 2014, local military officials violently evicted Garifuna communities from their Barra Vieja and Miami beachside villages. One community leader described the event in detail, explaining how members of the military woke him up and kicked him out of his home in the middle of the night. When he was able to return, his beachfront thatched-roof hut was completely leveled. The raids were meant to intimidate the community off their land, which is attractive real estate to Indura's expanding massive compound. In many cases, intimidation has proven successful; an estimated fifty thousand Garifuna people have migrated to the United States, with two to four thousand Garifuna people living in New Orleans.[19]

One of the few remaining hopes for the Barra Vieja community is its recognition as a historical site by the Tela Municipality since 1950, a status that gave Barra Vieja temporary reprieve from the local court after the 2014 raids. In 2015, the Inter-American Court of Human Rights (IACHR) ordered compensation for Garifuna land that was stolen and that more binding titles to the land be given to Garifuna people to better ensure protections. But little has been done to protect these lands and people because of the entrenched power of corporate interest coupled with the political limitations of organizations like UNESCO.[20]

While mainstream media's narratives of Central American migration tend to focus on gang violence, land annexation by tourism industries and palm oil plantations, often realized with state support, drive migration as well. Touted for the profits they'll bring to local communities, tourism development projects instead push people from their lands and threaten local communities. Nevertheless, deeming Garifuna land use unproductive and reinforcing job creation through the hotel industry provides justification for developments like Indura.

## A New Rebuilding?

The migratory paths that lead out of Honduras to cities like New Orleans enmesh these seemingly disparate locations, building upon one another in a transnational web of capital, goods, and people. Often thought of as destinations ripe with potential for touristic consumption, both New Orleans and coastal Honduras are much more than the commodified sum of their parts. Much of what makes New Orleans and northern Honduras attractive to tourists has been possible because of Black and Indigenous cultural production. Commodification erases and dilutes complex histories; ersatz gestures fail to preserve local practices. Using the word "Indura," which means "Honduras" in the Garifuna language, does nothing to mollify and only furthers the dispossession of the Garifuna people.

Nothing makes this erasure starker than the deportations, silencing of activists, and deaths of workers for the sake of crony capitalism. Victims of racial capitalism are connected to one another via multiracial organizing but also by local governments that bend to corporate interests, low-wage and unsafe work masquerading as "good jobs," residential displacement, lack of public investment, the silencing of dissent, and the construction of new buildings atop land sacred to local communities, whether referring to Garifuna ancestral land in Central America or the site of a seminal civil rights protest in New Orleans. Built environments expose the fact that extractive development projects are global in scope.

In Jamaica Kincaid's short 1988 memoir, *A Small Place*, she offers a scathing critique of tourist industries in her homeland of Antigua, a small island in the Caribbean. Kincaid is particularly critical of Antigua's Hotel Training School, arguing that it wants to teach "students how to be good servants." Kincaid posits, "In Antigua, people cannot see a relationship between their obsession with slavery and emancipation and their celebration of the Hotel Training School; people cannot see a relationship between their obsession with slavery and emancipation and the fact that they are governed by corrupt men, or that these corrupt men have given their country away to corrupt foreigners." In a 1991 interview, Kincaid explained how the Hotel Training School replaced Antigua's only Teacher's Training College, which can be interpreted as the unbuilding of an institution that made its local community strong.[21]

In the case of Kincaid's story, many of the workers, their families, and the land protectors had long been wary of the false promises of establishments like the Hotel Training School. Proponents of corporatist privatization perpetuate exploitative tourism industries at the expense of local people, culture, and economies. Emancipation histories are bulldozed, wages remain stagnant, inequality grows, and developers operate with no oversight.

Sergio, the brother of Ponce who was killed in the collapse, gives us an alternative to a new hotel: a park built in memory of the workers. As of March 30, 2021, and in the final stages of demolition, no plans for memorialization were underway. By integrating local histories, such a park could be a tribute to workers of all kinds, including the five individuals who sat at the counter at Woolworth's in defiance of segregation and Jim Crow. But efforts to redress injustices must go beyond symbolic parks and plaques. They must be built and rebuilt as policies—living wages, access to healthcare, worker protections, secure land titles—that better protect local communities from extractive economies on a global scale.[22] ◉

NOTES

1   "Brother of Jose Ponce Arreola Discusses Recovery of Remains," WWL-TV, August 18, 2020, https://www.wwltv.com/video/news/local/orleans/hard-rock-collapse/brother-of-jose-ponce-arreola-discusses-recovery-of-remains/289-3ac6d30a-74aa-42f6-aeaa-07f679536b5f.

2   Randy Gaspard, "Days Prior to Hard Rock Collapse, Citadel Well Aware of a Problem, Profits Over Safety, Sad!," Facebook, October 15, 2019, https://www.facebook.com/randy.gaspard.311/videos/17387067040289o/?t=8; Lee Zurik and Cody Lillich, "Zurik: Third City Inspector Likely Did Not Visit Hard Rock Site when He Signed Off on Work," Fox8live, last modified February 20, 2020, https://www.fox8live.com/2020/02/20/zurik-third-city-inspector-likely-did-not-visit-hard-rock-site-when-he-signed-off-work/; Jules Bentley, "Built to Kill: The Hard Rock Collapse Is Simply Business as Usual for Louisiana," *Antigravity*, November 2019, http://antigravitymagazine.com/feature/built-to-kill/.

3   Lynnell L. Thomas, *Desire and Disaster in New Orleans: Tourism, Race, and Historical Memory* (Durham, NC: Duke University Press, 2014); Deniz Daser, "Citizens of the City: Undocumented Latinx Migrants Organising Politically in Post-Katrina New Orleans," *Public Anthropologist* 3, no. 1 (March 2021): 148–176; Rachel Breunlin and Helen A. Regis, "Putting the Ninth Ward on the Map: Race, Place, and Transformation in Desire, New Orleans," *American Anthropologist* 108, no. 4 (December 2006): 744–764. Sarah Fouts is currently working on a book-length manuscript that explores these frameworks in greater depth.

4   Kirsten Silva Gruesz, "Converging Americas: New Orleans in Spanish-Language and Latina/o/x Literary Culture," in *New Orleans: A Literary History*, ed. T. R. Johnson (New York: Cambridge University Press, 2019), 137; George Lipsitz, *How Racism Takes Place* (Philadelphia: Temple University Press, 2011), 236–237; Neil Brenner and Nik Theodore, "Cities and the Geographies of 'Actually Existing Neoliberalism,'" *Antipode* 34, no. 3 (July 2002): 349–379. On racial capitalism, see Cedric J. Robinson, *Black Marxism: The Making of the Black Radical Tradition* (Chapel Hill: University of North Carolina Press, 1983).

5   "Kailas Companies | Real Estate Development & Management," Kailas Companies, accessed April 13, 2021, https://www.kailascompanies.com/; "Developer, Praveen Kailas, Sentenced to 30 Months for Theft of Government Funds and Conspiracy Charges," United States Department of Justice, December 18, 2013, https://www.justice.gov/usao-edla/pr/developer-praveen-kailas-sentenced-30-months-theft-government-funds-and-conspiracy; Timothy F. Green and Robert B. Olshansky, "Rebuilding Housing in New Orleans: the Road Home Program after the Hurricane Katrina Disaster," *Housing Policy Debate* 22, no. 1 (February 2012): 75–99; David Hammer, "Hard Rock Hotel Developer's Troubled Past First Exposed by WWL-TV," WWL-TV, October 16, 2019, https://www.wwltv.com/article/news/local/orleans/hard-rock-developer-had-troubled-past-exposed-by-wwl/289-834e15ba-3a60-4dff-9bbf-648d400565c5. In January 2020, Kailas was ordered by a judge to stop harassing tenants in a property he owned. Just a block away from the collapse, the thirty-one-story International Style skyscraper towers over the French Quarter, a stark contrast to the assemblage of wrought iron balconies, Creole cottages, and Greek Revivalist–style structures that give the Vieux Carre its charm. Kailas sought to vacate tenants who had occupied the high-rise property for over a decade in order to demolish the interior apartments and offices and make way for two more hotels. Anthony McAuley, "Stop Harassing Tenants at 1010 Common, Judge Orders Hard Rock Developer Kailas," *Times-Picayune*, January 24, 2020, https://www.nola.com/news/business/article_29c4d89e-3ed9-11ea-8802-07cdef30ed8e.html.

6   Michael Isaac Stein, "Hard Rock Developers Have Contributed Nearly $70,000 to Mayor Cantrell and Her Political Action Committee," Lens, January 28, 2020, https://thelensnola.org/2020/01/28/hard-rock-developers-have-contributed-nearly-70000-to-mayor-cantrell-and-her-political-action-committee/; McAuley, "Stop Harassing Tenants."

7 Richard Thompson, "Plans Unveiled for Hard Rock Hotel, New Orleans: 18 Floors, 350 Rooms on Canal Street," *Advocate*, February 15, 2018, https://www.nola.com/article_782b5dbc-9d2a-59e2-96a5-9b6048df5007.html; "Hard Rock International Plans French Quarter Hotel and Residences in 2019," Canal Street Beat, February 20, 2018, https://canalstreetbeat.com/hard-rock-international-plans-french-quarter-hotel-and-residences-in-2019/.

8 Leo B. Gorman, "Latino Migrant Labor Strife and Solidarity in Post-Katrina New Orleans, 2005–2007," *Latin Americanist* 54, no. 1 (March 2010): 1–33; A. L. Murga, "Organizing and Rebuilding a Nuevo New Orleans: Day Labor Organizing in the Big Easy," in *Working in the Big Easy: The History and Politics of Labor in New Orleans*, ed. Thomas J. Adams and Steve Striffler (Lafayette: University of Louisiana at Lafayette Press, 2014), 211–227; Daser, "Citizens of the City."

9 Erin Moore Daly, "New Orleans, Invisible City," *Nature and Culture* 1, no. 2 (Autumn 2006): 135; Rebecca Torres et al., "Building Austin, Building Justice: Immigrant Construction Workers, Precarious Labor Regimes and Social Citizenship," *Geoforum* 45 (March 2013): 147. In the twenty-year period between 1977 and 1997, the number of jobs in tourism went from 22,488 to 35,824, an increase of 60 percent. In the period between 1994 and 2002, hotel rooms in the city increased 40 percent. David Gladstone and Jolie Préau, "Gentrification in Tourist Cities: Evidence from New Orleans before and after Hurricane Katrina," *Housing Policy Debate* 19, no. 1 (2008): 140, 139. Globally, of the twenty-two (and eleven under construction) Hard Rock Hotels, only one, located in Atlantic City, is unionized. Robert Habans and Allison Plyer, "Benchmarking New Orleans' Tourism Economy: Hotel and Full-Service Restaurant Jobs," Data Center, December 2018, https://s3.amazonaws.com/gnocdc/reports/benchmarking-tourism-brief-habans-et-al.pdf.

10 Daser, "Citizens of the City"; Jade Scipioni, "NFL's Drew Brees Is Not Only a Passing Legend but also a Savvy Investor," Fox Business, October 9, 2018, https://www.foxbusiness.com/features/nfls-drew-brees-is-not-only-a-passing-legend-but-a-savvy-investor.

11 Deniz Daser, "Leveraging Labor in New Orleans: Worklife and Insecurity among Honduran Migrants" (PhD diss., Rutgers University, 2018).

12 John Burnett, "See the 20+ Immigration Activists Arrested under Trump," NPR, March 16, 2018, https://www.npr.org/2018/03/16/591879718/see-the-20-immigration-activists-arrested-under-trump. For more on deportability, see Daniel M. Goldstein and Carolina Alonso-Bejarano, "E-Terify: Securitized Immigration and Biometric Surveillance in the Workplace," *Human Organization* 76, no. 1 (Spring 2017): 1–14; and Nicholas P. De Genova, "Migrant 'Illegality' and Deportability in Everyday Life," *Annual Review of Anthropology* 31 (October 2002): 419–447.

13 Adam Davidson, "Who Wants to Buy Honduras?," *New York Times*, May 8, 2012, https://www.nytimes.com/2012/05/13/magazine/who-wants-to-buy-honduras.html; Naomi Klein, *The Shock Doctrine: The Rise of Disaster Capitalism* (New York: Henry Holt, 2007); Christopher A. Loperena, "Honduras Is Open for Business: Extractivist Tourism as Sustainable Development in the Wake of Disaster?," *Journal of Sustainable Tourism* 25, no. 5 (2017): 618–633; "Ten Years after the Honduran Coup: Selected Readings," North American Congress on Latin America, June 28, 2019, https://nacla.org/news/2019/06/28/ten-years-after-honduran-coup-selected-readings.

14 "Nestled Oceanside in Beautiful Tela Bay, Honduras," Indura Beach & Golf Resort, accessed April 14, 2021, http://induraresort.com/m/.

15 "Spa & Wellness," Indura Beach & Golf Resort, accessed April 14, 2021, http://www.induraresort.com/spa-wellness.html.

16 Loperena, "Honduras Is Open for Business."

17  Beth Geglia, "As Private Cities Advance in Honduras, Hondurans Renew Their Opposition," *Center for Economic and Policy Research* (blog), December 3, 2020, https://cepr.net/as-private-cities-advance-in-honduras-hondurans-renew-their-opposition/; Beth Geglia, "Honduras: Reinventing the Enclave," *NACLA Report on the Americas* 48, no. 4 (October 2016): 353–360; Nina Lakhani, "Honduras: Accused Mastermind of Berta Cáceres Murder to Go on Trial Next Month," *Guardian*, March 2, 2021, http://www.theguardian.com/world/2021/mar/02/berta-caceres-honduras-accused-mastermind-trial.

18  Anastasia Moloney, "Honduran Minority Fears for Survival after Leaders Abducted," Reuters, July 31, 2020, https://www.reuters.com/article/us-honduras-landrights-violence-trfn-idUSKCN-24W1OG.

19  Interview with Garifuna community leader conducted during Sarah Fouts's fieldwork to Barra Vieja and the Atlántida region of Honduras in July 2015. Population numbers for the Garifuna people in the United States are hard to track based on census data because Garifuna don't fit the rigid identity structure of census formats. James Chaney's work cites an estimate from 1997 for the New Orleans data on Garifuna people in New Orleans; however, the numbers are likely much higher. Nationwide statistics approximate one hundred thousand people. For New Orleans Garifuna information, see James Chaney, "Malleable Identities: Placing the Garínagu in New Orleans," *Journal of Latin American Geography* 11, no. 2 (2012): 128. For information on Garifuna in New York, see David Gonzalez, "Garifuna Immigrants in New York," *Lens* (blog), July 24, 2015, https://lens.blogs.nytimes.com/2015/07/24/garifuna-immigrants-in-new-york/. For information on Garifuna and the US census, see "Garifuna and the 2020 Census," *PhilanTopic* (blog), Candid, December 2, 2019, https://pndblog.typepad.com/pndblog/2019/12/garifunas-and-the-2020-census.html.

20  James Rodríguez, "Garifuna Resistance against Mega-Tourism in Tela Bay," North American Congress on Latin America, August 5, 2008, https://nacla.org/news/garifuna-resistance-against-mega-tourism-tela-bay; "The Garifuna Community of Barra Vieja on Trial for Defending Ancestral Territory," Latin America in Movement, April 6, 2015, https://www.alainet.org/en/articulo/170135?language=en; Proah, "The Garifuna Community of Barra Vieja on Trial for Defending Ancestral Territory," Latin America in Movement, April 6, 2015, https://www.alainet.org/en/articulo/170135?language=en.

21  Jamaica Kincaid, *A Small Place* (New York: Farrar, Straus and Giroux, 1988), 55; Allan Vorda and Jamaica Kincaid, "An Interview with Jamaica Kincaid," *Mississippi Review* 20, no. 1/2 (1991): 7–26.

22  Jeff Adelson and Jessica Williams, "The Hard Rock Hotel Collapsed 17 Months Ago; Now Demolition Nears Its End," NOLA, March 30, 2021, https://www.nola.com/news/politics/article_8ae71346-91b0-11eb-a2f8-67fa982790f9.html. For information on how other activist groups have suggested a similar way of memorializing, see Justin Montrie, "Call for Public Hearing on the Hard Rock Hotel Disaster | Call for a Community Rights Park," Change.org, accessed August 30, 2020, https://www.change.org/p/the-people-call-for-public-hearings-on-the-hard-rock-hotel-collapse-this-is-a-call-for-a-community-rights-memorial-park-at-1031-1041-canal.

# Eating Dirt, Searching Archives

Excavations from a Texas Woman

*by* Endia L. Hayes // *illustrations by* Natalie Nelson

For when your judgments are in the earth, the inhabitants of the world learn righteousness.

— Isaiah 26:9

Eat *ēt* (v): to destroy, consume, or waste by or as if by eating; to bear the expense of; to enjoy eagerly or avidly; to affect something by gradual destruction or consumption.

— *Merriam-Webster*

**LAND OF THE SWEET,** never sour, Sugar Land, Texas, offers a surburban alternative outside the expanding Houston area.[1]

The city has gone by many names. In 1838, two years into the Republic of Texas's victory over the Republic of Mexico, what is now Sugar Land was named the Oakland Plantation. Stephen F. Austin (the "Father of Texas") gave land to businessman and administrator Samuel May Williams as payment for his work providing land grants as incentives to bring white settlers to the new republic. In 1853, Williams sold the plantation to his brothers, Nathaniel and Matthew Williams. Together, they combined the plantation with adjoining lands and renamed it Sugar Land. The late 1800s brought a new nickname to Sugar Land among the city's convict laborers: "Hell Hole on the Brazos." Sugar Land's infrastructure expanded in the decades following the end of convict leasing in 1912, resulting in the erasure of the city's histories of Black and Indigenous removal. The city's wealth — held almost exclusively by its white business owners, former plantation owners, and political elites — grew thanks to sugar tours, school field trips to the humid banks of the Brazos River, and the wealth generated by sugar production. These legacies of violence, swallowed by the earth and long buried, were unearthed in 2018 when developers disturbed the dirt underneath the city.[2]

Texas has buried its history rather well. Sugar Land is land of the Karankawa and Tonkawa tribes, which gathered at the now commercial banks of Sugar Land's Oyster Creek and Brazos River. Oakland Plantation began with Indigenous removal and the sinister capitalism that maintained brutal control over Black bodies forced to do hard labor. These were the legacies of plantation violence and its afterlives during the Civil War and Reconstruction.[3]

The Williams brothers used Oyster Creek to build a commercial sugar mill, and on Oakland Plantation they forced enslaved people to harvest sugarcane. After the area had been renamed Sugar Land, the city's penal system began under former Confederate colonel Edward H. Cunningham (also known as the "Texas Sugar King"). It was during this time, when convicts were leased out to work privately owned land, that Sugar Land became known as the Hell Hole on the Brazos. Over the years, more and more privately owned plantation land was transferred to

the state, a profitable move that allowed Texas to maintain the city's economic growth while continuing to benefit from the people generating that growth: Black prison laborers.[4]

Much of the state's Black history remains difficult to find, often having been relegated to small rural museums. Not to mention that the narrative Texas condones in its education system neglects discussion of enslavement, plantation lives, and prison farms. But Black Texas offers alternative archives mostly unreliant on documents and museum space. These alternatives thrive in orality, testimony, folklore, music—and dirt.[5]

In April 2018, construction workers came across ninety-five sets of remains at the site of what was intended to be the $59 million career and technical center for Fort Bend Independent School District (FBISD). This piece of land under construction was once the Imperial Sugar Company headquarters. Fort Bend County and its neighboring counties, Matagorda, Wharton, and Brazoria, formed the "Sugar Bowl of Texas" for centuries courtesy of the Williams brothers. It is estimated that the people in this unmarked cemetery, estimated to have been buried between 1878 and 1911, ranged from fourteen to seventy years old when they died. Their discovery immediately interrupted the construction of FBISD's center. *Washington Post* reporter Meagan Flynn noted that signs of "repetitive wear" engraved on each of these Black bodies "indicat[ed] hard labor." That wear marked the statewide funding of plantations-turned-prison-farms for Black convicts.[6]

To recognize that we have been living alongside the dead means reshaping our relationship to Texas dirt. The breadth of Black death, unearthed, shifts how we understand Black Texas histories in Sugar Land. Katherine McKittrick describes the built knowledge and geographies that we find ourselves bound to as "familiar plot[s]." But looking beneath Sugar Land's built environment—one that thrives on consumption and neglect—allows us to imagine the city in a different way. The history of sugar's infrastructure cannot exist apart from state-sanctioned violence, apart from engraved shackles on flesh. By looking at Texas dirt anew, I wish to explore what it has meant for me and other Black Texans to confront this place's haunting by former prison laborers and plantation slaves. What is the vantage point of the dead and what is their history? In its quest for an empire built on sugar, Sugar Land has consumed Black flesh and buried its remains in its infrastructure under the guise of progress. But dirt preserved the visceral realities of early Black life in Sugar Land. Unearthing what Sugar Land's dirt holds brings Texas's invisible geographies to light, allowing us to imagine an alternative archive made over time in Sugar Land. New ways of knowing emerge when we dig below Sugar Land's industrial legacies—when, instead of eating the sugar it produces, we consume the contents of the city's underground archive. My own memories, and the markings of the prison laborers, demand this shift.[7]

**I WAS CALLED TO THE GROUND** early in life. Ground was familiar, a source of meaning-making present in family stories, a reminder under my fingernails of learning how to unearth potatoes and peas, a lingering trace in pots of greens. Yet, my grandfather told me that the ground was not ours, that what was once our legacy had been taken, bought, and stripped. Ground—and, more specifically, dirt—was contentious for me, an idea that Katherine McKittrick illuminates: "If the earth has skin, then the dirt is its memory." The discovery of the Sugar Land 95 moved me toward a deeper understanding of Texas memory.[8]

For seven years, I attended a private Christian high school in Sugar Land. The Imperial Sugar Company was a three or so minute drive from the school, and I remember staring at the large building immediately behind the railroad tracks off Highway 90. It was abandoned but the huge Imperial Sugar Factory sign remained. I have used that brand of sugar in cooking, baking, and memory-making. I was curious about what it looked like inside, who worked there, what stories it held. What would this factory tell me about the history of the sugar I used? In 2015, there were whispers that the land on which the Imperial Sugar Factory stood might be torn down to make room for an advanced technical center for surrounding high schools (many of which are predominantly white). My school community was excited about the possibility of witnessing its destruction (while planning last tours, last observances). With each drive past the sign, I savored what I believed to be my final views of its mystery. But amid this place's troublesome grounds, I continued to eat dirt, uncertain whether I would find Black Texas history in Sugar Land.

The discovery of the Sugar Land 95, as they came to be known, uncovered a new sense of Texas space. Dirt has been a means of sustenance, cultivated and contested, a site of economic and ideological possession—but the 95 necessitated an alternate reading of Sugar Land's spatial origins. Dirt is what sociologist Avery F. Gordon calls a "social figure," a haunting presence that exists in the intimate margins between life and death. The dirt is messy, revealing much of what I do not know while also revealing that I know too much about my home space. Digging in the dirt and reflecting upon this city space showed me that my Blackness did not belong. Digging meant unburying the lie that enslavement did not reach Texas. Two years of required Texas history across middle and high school failed to teach us that Black Texans were the last to know that slavery had ended, a moment now marked by the annual celebration of Juneteenth. In fact, I learned about Juneteenth celebrations in communion with my family,

when we sat at picnic tables outside, bare feet shuffling in red dirt, and ate barbecued ribs and pieces of brisket. Those experiences built a history separate from the one advertised by Fort Bend County and its private schools. When I entered graduate school, I attempted to make my own archive focused on learning about enslavement along the Gulf Coast. I never looked farther west than Louisiana; I didn't know that Southeast Texas was known for its sugar cane  production. Little is known of those sugar plantations my parents' home now sits on, the ground I walked for school, or the dirt my toddler sister and brother once found so enjoyable to consume unknowingly. Dirt archives the lives of the buried, preserving their difficult truths and complicating, if not dismantling, dominant histories built above ground. Dirt allows me to see beneath Texas history to recover the stories of the wronged and forgotten.[9]

This mass grave site contained not just the misshapen bones of prison laborers, but also those of the formerly enslaved. According to news reports, many bodies were buried in chains and with the tools of their livelihoods. As I speculate about the unspoken lives of those bones, I imagine a girl or woman—perhaps only fourteen—sent to labor on a plantation. What do her misshapen bones and shackled ankles show us about Texas afterlives? Now, upon the discovery of her abused and abandoned body, what can we understand? The years between 1878 and 1911, when the bodies were buried, were formative in Texas's convict leasing system and sugar cane production, both key in sustaining the state's sugar wealth following the legal eradication of the plantation system. The bodies that rested in Texas dirt reveal the underbelly of this history of wealth and progress. Contorted bones evidence violence and exhaustion. Perhaps the bones of the woman or girl I imagine reveal gendered violence that occurred under the demands of "Texas Sugar King" Cunningham, notorious for making Sugar Land the Hell Hole. Dirt both hid the remains of the 95 and protected their stories.[10]

When I think back, I wonder if my body knew something that I had yet to understand but had already consumed. I recall the land I've traversed over the years—for field trips, for family visits, for work and leisure—and how my own body and its memories have been shaped by this place, from what I chose to hold in my hands to what my family told me to wash, peel, shuck, dig up, and bury. These are the sources of wonder and curiosity I sought to remember as I worked through the disruption of Sugar Land's dirt. It was an opportunity bestowed by ancestors, mine and others, to unsettle not only linear ideas of Texas history but also the built environment as a means of erasure. This dirt is porous, but it's also densely packed. It is a source

of what scholar Tiffany Lethabo King calls a "flexible analytic . . . a mode of critique and an alternative reading practice." Dirt is a container, a way to hold memory. The painful experience of reading this city's dirt, the Sugar Land 95's contorted bones, and the difficult truths I imagine for a girl or woman, offers me a framework for understanding the buried history of violence that went into making Sugar Land. Though these lives will in some ways always continue to dwell in the ground, their stories are being unearthed.[11]

The 2018 dig is a reminder that all the joy I locate in Texas soil—as a consumer, lover, and wanderer—required intimate engagement with Black death in the Hell Hole on the Brazos. The land developed for Texas's eighteenth- and nineteenth-century economies reflects a violence that relegates Black bodies to the dirt, then literally builds on them, for the sake of progress and profit. This progress would overwrite enslavement and its afterlives altogether. There are numerous unmarked graves, burials, and bodies gone to dust and countless histories interred in the land. The Sugar Land 95 remind us that those gone to dust still reside in the dirt—and that the flesh that becomes dirt is not only a memory embedded in the land but also an archive providing access to that memory. Dirt offers Black Texas a tangible afterlife. It is intelligible only to those whose flesh is familiar with it, who feel it in their bodies, who have consumed it or are deeply connected to it. Dirt preserves Black Texas life, even in its density.

Scholar L. H. Stallings writes that dirt is a "tool, ingredient, or craft material . . . a conductor of sacred energy." I surmise that Texas dirt reveals difficult truths, one of which is Texas's legacy of carcerality. Dirt offers an alternative epistemology—one that outlives the region's many structures perpetuating violence and historical erasures. Dirt also negates material archives (documents, photos, infrastructural memorialization of the Alamo, plaques along the Brazos, and statewide social science curricula that often erase Indigenous and Black Texas life) as the sole means to advance knowledge of Texas and its origins. *Wear it down*, dirt seems to say. In time, dirt reveals what it holds. This alternative epistemology asks us to start with the bare soil. Its memories, dense flesh, what it knows and how it can heal, demand that we engage in the messy practice of unearthing. My encounters with Texas dirt allow me to remember differently. In this archive, Black Texan folks—who continue to communicate even in death—are whole enough to be properly remembered as humans who had feelings, wanted to love and be loved, desired freedom, and grew abundant community alongside sugar. Sugar Land has long presented a façade, but it has always been the Hell Hole on the Brazos for the 95. The sugar economy—its mills, factories, the neighborhoods and tours that it made possible—was a multilayered concrete cover built over histories of sugar, violence, and Black labor.[12]

The ground, in and of itself, has too often been excluded from discussions of southern enslavement, despite emerging work on Black ecologies and geographies. But, here, dirt serves as a text that allows us to chronicle Black life under settler colonialism. When we eat dirt, we practice unearthing alternative archives—of memories, past lives, legacies, and afterlives. We also resist more destructive forms of consumption. There are many Black afterlives that have yet to be unearthed.[13]

Today, what was once an unknown mass grave is now the Bullhead Camp Cemetery. The Sugar Land 95 have been given proper burials with individual caskets, a public ceremony, and newly dedicated tour grounds for public visits—all with the city's promise that this dirt will serve as a reminder and a lesson for the communitty. And I sense that Texas dirt still has more to tell. ◐

---

NOTES

1   *Merriam-Webster*, s.v. "eat (*v.*)," accessed April 10, 2021, https://www.merriam-webster.com/dictionary/eat.

2   Eugene C. Barker, "Stephen Fuller Austin," Texas State Cemetery, accessed April 10, 2021, https://cemetery.tspb.texas.gov/pub/user_form.asp?pers_id=3; "Sugar Land: Historical Timeline," City of Sugar Land, accessed April 10, 2021, http://www.sugarlandtx.gov/1773/Sugar-Land-Historical-Timeline; Michael Hardy, "Blood and Sugar," *Texas Monthly*, January 2017, https://www.texasmonthly.com/articles/sugar-land-slave-convict-labor-history/. See also Andrea R. Roberts, "Haunting as Agency: A Critical Cultural Landscape Approach to Making Black Labor Visible in Sugar Land, Texas," *ACME* 19, no. 1 (2020): 210–244.

3   Hanna Kim, "Unearthing Truth: The Future of Sugar Land, Texas Depends on Its Bitter Past," DES 3333: Culture, Conservation and Design, 2018, https://higherlogicdownload.s3.amazonaws.

com/SAVINGPLACES/UploadedImages/23769d2e-1cf3-4995-b107-58280aeb6b76/Sugar_Land/Final_Paper_by_Hanna_Kim.pdf. For a discussion of Sugar Land's Indigenous roots, see "Sugar Land: Historical Timeline"; Carol Lipscomb, "Karankawa Indians," Texas State Historical Association, accessed April 14, 2021, https://www.tshaonline.org/handbook/entries/karankawa-indians; and Jeffrey D. Carlisle, "Tonkawa Indians," Texas State Historical Association, accessed April 14, 2021, https://www.tshaonline.org/handbook/entries/tonkawa-indians.

4   "Sugar Land"; Convict Leasing and Labor Project, accessed April 14, 2021, https://www.cllptx.org.

5   For more on the erasure of enslavement in Texas education, please see Manny Fernandez and Christine Hauser, "Texas Mother Teaches Textbook Company a Lesson on Accuracy," *New York Times*, October 5, 2015, https://www.nytimes.com/2015/10/06/us/publisher-promises-revisions-after-textbook-refers-to-african-slaves-as-workers.html; Michael Brick, "Texas School Board Set to Vote Textbook Revisions," *New York Times*, May 20, 2010, https://www.nytimes.com/2010/05/21/education/21textbooks.html; and Kritika Agarwal, "Texas Revises History Education, Again: How a 'Good Faith' Process Became Political," *Perspectives on History*, January 11, 2019, https://www.historians.org/publications-and-directories/perspectives-on-history/january-2019/texas-revises-history-education-again-how-a-good-faith-process-became-political.

6   Hardy, "Blood and Sugar"; Meagan Flynn, "Bodies Believed to Be Those of 95 Black Forced-Labor Prisoners from Jim Crow Era Unearthed in Sugar Land after One Man's Quest," *Washington Post*, July 18, 2018, https://www.washingtonpost.com/news/morning-mix/wp/2018/07/18/bodies-of-95-black-forced-labor-prisoners-from-jim-crow-era-unearthed-in-sugar-land-after-one-mans-quest/; Matthew Clarke, "Texas Convict-Leasing Burial Ground Uncovered," *Prison Legal News*, January 8, 2020, https://www.prisonlegalnews.org/news/2020/jan/8/texas-convict-leasing-burial-ground-uncovered/.

7   Katherine McKittrick, *Demonic Grounds: Black Women and the Cartographies of Struggle* (Minneapolis: University of Minnesota, 2006), 127. Grappling to mediate my personal life in Sugar Land and the brutality that marked the uncovered bodies of the incarcerated and enslaved allowed me to think alongside scholars who speak to Texas's haunting; see Roberts, "Haunting as Agency."

8   McKittrick, *Demonic Grounds*, ix.

9   Avery F. Gordon, *Ghostly Matters: Haunting and the Sociological Imagination* (Minneapolis: University of Minnesota Press, 2008), 8.

10  Flynn, "Bodies Believed."

11  Tiffany Lethabo King, "The Labor of (Re)reading Plantation Landscapes Fungible(ly)," *Antipode* 48, no. 4 (March 2016): 1023.

12  L. H. Stallings, *A Dirty South Manifesto: Sexual Resistance and Imagination in the New South* (Oakland: University of California Press, 2020), 38–39.

13  Recent scholarship on Black ecologies and Black geographies engages the metaphorical and symbolic role of the southern soil. Some of this work around the relationship between Black life, enslavement, and settler colonialism includes Kathryn Yusoff, *A Billion Black Anthropecenes or None* (Minneapolis: University of Minnesota Press, 2018); Clyde Woods, *Development Arrested: The Blues and Plantation Power in the Mississippi Delta*, 2nd. ed. (New York: Verso, 2017); Katherine McKittrick and Clyde Woods, *Black Geographies and the Politics of Place* (Cambridge, MA: South End, 2007); Andrea Roberts and M. J. Biazar, "Black Placemaking in Texas: Sonic and Social Histories of Newton and Jasper County Freedom Colonies," *Current Research in Digital History*, no. 2 (2019); "Introducing a New Series on Black Ecologies," *Black Perspectives* (blog), African American Intellectual History Society, June 16, 2020, https://www.aaihs.org/introducing-the-black-ecologies-series/; J. T. Roane, "Plotting the Black Commons," *Souls* 20, no. 3 (2018): 239–266; and Fred Moten and Saidiya Hartman, "Fred Moten & Saidiya Hartman at Duke University | The Black Outdoors," Duke Franklin Humanities Institute, October 5, 2016, YouTube video, 2:04:02, https://www.youtube.com/watch?v=t_tUZ6dybrc. These works only begin to scratch the surface of emerging studies of Black relations to ground, particularly in the legacy of settler colonialism and the plantation.

# Latter-Day Paradises in the Cherokee National Forest

## I.

Geographer Dennis Cosgrove has written that American landscapes may best be apprehended from the air. So vast are US landscapes and, likewise, our interventions to rework them, that a vantage point at that level of remove is necessary to appreciate the scale of physical and human geographies here. Nowhere, perhaps, is that perspective more apposite to grasp the enormity of planned American landscapes than for the series of behemoth, high-modern, dirigiste projects undertaken by the Tennessee Valley Authority (TVA), whose territory, spanning seven states, is half the size of California.[1]

*photographs by* **John Lusk Hathaway**
*introduced by* **Mark Long**

Little Milligan, Tennessee, 2011.

Little Stony Creek, Tennessee, 2011.

Close to a century after its creation, in the fading years of the last generation to marvel at the miracle of instantaneous light and energy, the magnitude of those engineering projects is as taken for granted as the electricity that is one of the TVA's lasting legacies for millions across the South. Yet, for all that the exercise of colossal governmental power and the monumental transformations that result are often overlooked today, their impact on the ground is plain to see in John Lusk Hathaway's photography project *One Foot in Eden*.[2]

Hathaway's subjects are, most immediately, day-trippers to the Cherokee National Forest, along waterways repurposed as a network of reservoirs under the TVA, on the border between North Carolina and Tennessee. Many arrive from nearby Johnson City and some, likely, are descended from the very people displaced from these hills and valleys as dams were built in the twentieth century. They come to hike, to picnic, to boat, to hunt and fish; most of them, according to the Forest Service, from within fifty miles. More men than women, nearly all

Little Stony Creek,
Tennessee, 2011.

Hampton, Tennessee, 2011.

of the visitors are white, a reflection of local demographics and the underrepresentation of minority populations in national parks countrywide.[3]

Key to Hathaway's explorations is a paradox: enormous expanses of the South have been preserved and remain undeveloped precisely because they were originally subjugated for regional development. Regional planning, in places like the South, often meant that designs for governmental interventions were as grand as the places they would transform. Unlike so many tracts of land elsewhere, given over to the banality of urbanization, suburbanization, and exurbanization in the creation of endless geographies of nowhere, here development meant dams, reservoirs, and hydroelectric power. Decades later, the resulting landscapes open windows onto nature as it has always been, even if, as these photographs attest, it is now framed by high-tension electrical cables and the other interminable straight lines that delineate modernity itself.[4]

Hughes Gap, Tennessee, 2011.

The people that populate Hathaway's images rest and recreate among massive infrastructures and the tendrils that link them into the networks of the modern world. They take in the vastness of the panoramas before them, yet experience the intimacy of being grounded in the materiality of water, earth, wood, stone, and fresh air, far from the humdrum noise of lives lived elsewhere. Beholding these hills, valleys, forests, and waterways in Appalachia is a conduit to a primordial past.

Much more than mere recreation, time in the outdoors is an essential dimension of the human condition, and the people pictured here draw on a deep primal well when they return, time and again, to cherished spots along the waterways of the Cherokee National Forest. Hathaway's photographs reflect the natural landscapes that were our habitat for 99 percent of our history as a species, yet we feel the transience of the moments his images capture, with but one foot in Eden.[5]

Little Stony Creek, Tennessee, 2011.

## II.

Deep-seated connections to the world around us can be described in terms of biophilia, the idea that humans are primed to value themselves as part of larger biological realities. Coined by biologist E. O. Wilson, biophilia would recognize certain landscapes as universal constants in cultures worldwide. Among them are places overlooking the savanna, woodlands, and, tellingly for Hathaway's enterprise, places where water is found.[6]

Beyond the necessity of obtaining food, water, and shelter, researchers verify that natural landscapes are good for the soul, likely resulting from an innate need for the calm required for emotional well-being, recovery from fatigue, stress relief, and, perhaps, creative problem-solving. And even unspectacular natural environments can work the magic of medicine for healthy individuals, as well as those in convalescence, leading, for surgery patients, to lower numbers of days of inpatient postoperative care, fewer negative evaluative comments

Hampton, Tennessee, 2011.

in nurses' reports, and lower prescription rates for painkillers. Time spent in this Eden, then, is a restorative salve for Hathaway's subjects, impacting everything from heart rate to brain activity to immune system responses.[7]

The ritual of returning to these places may also faintly echo migratory patterns whereby kin groups moved with the seasons, and over longer time horizons as well, making their way back to traditional sites. Just as our ancestors tracked their food, the examples of hunting and fishing that we see in Hathaway's photographs speak to sustenance from the forest, an aspect reaffirmed in the many images of families and friends preparing and consuming food. The demeanor of the visitors in repose and reverie foregrounds these as nurturing landscapes.[8]

Rituals are encoded here in multiple ways, calling attention to this place's spiritual dimensions. T-shirts, shorts, and flip-flops repeat across the photographs so often as to suggest an understated uniform for this wilderness. Time spent in and around the water is a constant:

Tiger Creek, Tennessee, 2011.

along the shore, on boats, wading and drifting, basking in the sun. There are images of dams in the forest, but TVA infrastructure is obliquely pictured in this project, as in photographs of drowned trees and stumps made visible as water is drawn down for hydroelectricity generation and as periodic droughts lower the waterline across these valleys.[9]

Johnson City, Tennessee, 2014.

Those droughts are of a piece with the flood events that again loom within the TVA system under climate change. Our stewardship of microcosmic arcadias like the Cherokee National Forest begs questions about our relationship to other paradises, most pressingly Earth as our only home. Ultimately, Hathaway's project asks us to consider the urgency of our present moment and whether we're stepping into or out of our Edens.[10] ⑤

Wiseman Branch, Tennessee, 2011.

← Lakeshore Marina, Tennessee, 2011.

Wilbur Lake, Tennessee, 2011.

Hampton, Tennessee, 2011.

Cardens Bluff, Tennessee, 2011.

NOTES

1   Denis Cosgrove, *Geography and Vision: Seeing, Imagining and Representing the World* (New York: I. B. Tauris, 2008).

2   John Lusk Hathaway, "One Foot in Eden," accessed April April 6, 2021, http://www.johnluskhathaway.com/welcome/uncategorized/one-foot-in-eden/.

3   United States Department of Agriculture Forest Service, *Visitor Use Report Cherokee NF*, last modified February 2, 2021, https://apps.fs.usda.gov/nvum/results/ReportCache/2017_A08004_Master_Report.pdf; Carolyn Finney, *Black Faces, White Spaces: Reimagining the Relationship of African Americans to the Great Outdoors* (Chapel Hill: University of North Carolina Press, 2014).

4   Patrick Kline and Enrico Moretti, "Local Economic Development, Agglomeration Economies, and the Big Push: 100 Years of Evidence from the Tennessee Valley Authority," *Quarterly Journal of Economics* 129, no. 1 (February 2014): 275–331; James Howard Kunstler, *The Geography of Nowhere: The Rise and Decline of America's Man-Made Landscape* (New York: Simon and Schuster, 1994).

5   Edward O. Wilson, *Biophilia: The Human Bond with Other Species* (Cambridge, MA: Harvard University Press, 1984); Judith H. Heerwagen and Gordon H. Orians, "Humans, Habitats, and Aesthetics," in *The Biophilia Hypothesis*, ed. Stephen R. Kellert and Edward O. Wilson (Washington, DC: Shearwater, 1993), 138–172.

6   Wilson, *Biophilia*.

7   Roger S. Ulrich, "Biophilia, Biophobia, and Natural Landscapes," in *The Biophilia Hypothesis*, ed. Stephen R. Kellert and Edward O. Wilson (Washington, DC: Shearwater, 1993), 73–137; Roger S. Ulrich, "View through a Window May Influence Recovery from Surgery," *Science* 224, no. 4647 (April 1984): 420–421; Florence Williams, *The Nature Fix: Why Nature Makes Us Happier, Healthier, and More Creative* (New York: Norton, 2017).

8   Marcus J. Hamilton et al., "The Ecological and Evolutionary Energetics of Hunter-Gatherer Residential Mobility," *Evolutionary Anthropology* 25, no. 3 (May 2016): 124–132.

9   Lucy R. Lippard, *The Lure of the Local: Senses of Place in a Multicentered Society* (New York: New Press, 2007).

10  Tennessee Valley Authority, *Climate Change Adaptation and Resiliency Plan 2020 Update*, July 15, 2020, https://tva-azr-eastus-cdn-ep-tvawcm-prd.azureedge.net/cdn-tvawcma/docs/default-source/about-tva/guidelines-reports/climate-change-adaptation-plan.pdf?sfvrsn=ea883571_2. See also Sarah Kennedy and ChavoBart Digital Media, "Ancient Tennessee River Floods Hold a Warning for the Future," Yale Climate Connections, Yale School of the Environment, accessed April 6, 2021, https://yaleclimateconnections.org/2020/08/ancient-tennessee-river-floods-hold-a-warning-for-the-future/.

# The Lake and the Landfill

In Search of Atlanta's Lake Charlotte

*by* Hannah S. Palmer *// illustrations by* Nate Beaty

**L**AKE CHARLOTTE STARTED to bother me one summer while I was working on a freelance project with a nonprofit called Trees Atlanta. Somewhere in the organization's sunny building, I saw a poster illustrating Atlanta's tree canopy—a kind of heat map of trees that needed saving. Red-orange blocks downtown sprawled into yellow-green neighborhoods and green parks. I studied it while waiting for my meeting to begin, amused to see the typical city map in reverse, defined by its undeveloped pockets instead of highways. The deepest green was in the southeast corner of the city, an emerald parcel bounded by a landfill and I-285. I knew what it was—Lake Charlotte Nature Preserve—but I had never been there.

According to this map, the forest was larger and greener than Piedmont Park and Grant Park combined. I tried to picture it and came up blank. All I remembered was the forbidding landfills and barren truck lots clustered in the elbow of the interstate. Old junkyards, strip clubs, and public housing projects scattered along Moreland Avenue. Long before I knew about zoning, I recognized the land-use pattern that sited poor Black neighborhoods alongside industrial districts. For most of my life, I had avoided this area, home, apparently, to the single largest concentration of intact tree canopy left inside the city limits.

As a Southside native and a generally outdoorsy mom, I was embarrassed by this gap in my mental map of Atlanta. I would rectify this immediately. Take the kids for a sweaty ramble around the lake and document it on Instagram. This weekend. But as I mapped out our first trip to Lake Charlotte, only eight miles from home, I couldn't find any information on the city Office of Parks website. No photos or trail reviews, only curious explorers sharing rumors on message boards. There were places where you could sneak through the fence, they said, but no public access.

All the maps were wrong. They showed Lake Charlotte Nature Preserve as a green rectangle with a thin, whale-shaped lake in the center. The blunt face of the whale must have been a dam once, its body a flooded valley. But the satellite image showed a meadow, no lake. Stymied by these findings, I let summer turn to fall, then the holidays arrived without an expedition to Lake Charlotte. A couple more summers went by. Every time I saw it labeled falsely on a map, it bothered me more. Was it ever a public park? Who was Charlotte and what happened to her lake? And just what was behind that fence?

**THE RECENT HISTORY OF THE LAND** was easy to find online in property records and local news sites. Fulton County listed Lake Charlotte's owner as Waste Management, Inc., same owner of the adjacent parcel in DeKalb County, the monumental Live Oak landfill. Live Oak opened in 1986 and it bought the forest next door in 1989, anticipating future expansion.[1]

Live Oak always struck me as a comical name for a dump, devoid, as it was, of trees and living things. As a child in the '90s, commuting between my dad's and mom's houses, I learned to crank up my car window as soon as I spotted the grassy ziggurat that loomed on the horizon and punctured the dark with spooky blue flares. But even with the window up, the sour milk stink of the dump lingered in the car well past businesses like Hub Cap Daddy and The Foxy Lady.

I remember reading about the controversy surrounding the landfill. It was located in DeKalb County, but the smell traveled for miles, into neighboring Atlanta and Clayton County neighborhoods, where residents gradually stopped hosting backyard cookouts, stopped leaving their windows open at night. In 1993, when Waste Management applied for a permit to expand into the Lake Charlotte property, Atlanta residents—most of them Black working-class homeowners—organized in protest. Live Oak was one of several enormous "solid waste handling facilities" already dominating Southeast Atlanta and southwest DeKalb County. The city denied the permit and residents celebrated.[2]

Instead of expanding outward, the landfill rose like a loaf of bread—a rotten rectangle squeezed straight by the county line and the interstate. The Lake Charlotte property was the only buffer between the reeking dump and backyards in South River Gardens, a predominantly Black neighborhood. By 2000, Live Oak started accepting "sludge," a byproduct of sewage treatment plants that is typically converted to fertilizer, and the smell became unbearable. Live Oak's waste handling was both sloppy and illegal, which ignited further protests.[3]

Southwest DeKalb residents appealed to their legislators and rallied at the state capitol, framing their burden as a case of environmental racism. In 2003, when Georgia's Environmental Protection Division finally ordered Live Oak to shut down operations, the landfill was already full to capacity and over a decade past its original life expectancy. In 2007, Waste Management started harvesting methane from the capped landfill, but held onto Lake Charlotte. For decades, the two hundred–acre Lake Charlotte property remained undisturbed and mislabeled on maps, a forgotten forest with a padlock on the fence.[4]

**I HAD TO DIG INTO** the city's planning documents from the late seventies, comprehensive plans and land-use plans and annual reports from the Bureau of Parks and Rec with sexy typography and optimistic sketches, to find proof that, once upon a time, briefly, Lake Charlotte Nature Preserve was exactly what it sounded like: a public park with a lake in the center.

This inner-city campground was the brainchild of Ted Mastroianni, Mayor Maynard Jackson's "fast moving and aggressive" director of parks and recreation. Recruited from New York City's parks department, he joined Mayor Jackson's team in 1975 and declared they would be "balancing the park system," by acquiring and protecting half a dozen wooded tracts across the Southside. "What seems to excite Mastroianni the most," according to the *Atlanta Constitution*, "is the acquisition of natural open spaces." In the 1975 annual report, he appears with bushy hair and a double chin over his wide necktie and lapels, captured mid-laugh so you can see his molars. He was only thirty-six years old.[5]

"We want areas where you can walk and lose yourself, rather than having to drive two hours to the North Georgia mountains," Mastroianni told the reporter. "If we develop good parks

and campsites inside the cities, maybe people will stop hating the cities." I could picture this young New Yorker flying into Atlanta, gazing down upon the Southside with that big grin. From a planner's eye view, it seemed like a great idea to preserve these forests before they were swallowed by development. In 1977, Mastroianni marshaled federal and state grants to purchase

Instead of expanding outward, the landfill rose like a loaf of bread—a rotten rectangle squeezed straight by the county line and the interstate.

the placid ten-acre Lake Charlotte and forty acres surrounding it. He told reporters that the park would be "open as soon as the paperwork is completed." When Mastroianni said, "Practically no improvements are required. It just becomes a park," he underestimated what it would take to make an inner-city wilderness feel appealing and safe.[6]

Despite these visionary investments in the city's park system, by the 1980s, the area was at a tipping point. Growing landfills and declining public housing projects surrounded Lake Charlotte. There's a term for infrastructure and industrial sites like landfills that nobody wants in their backyard—LULU, or locally undesirable land use. DeKalb County was committed to stashing industrial LULUS here, near I-285 and the new interstate bypass I-675, a development trend that eventually eclipsed Mastroianni's idea of a fun family getaway.[7]

In 1986, the city scrapped the entire project, saying that "the unattended nature of the park attracts illicit acts." They sold the land at a loss to a private developer named Herman Lischkoff. I struggled to imagine the context—the crisis, really—in which such a disposal of public lands could be done without scandal. But the more I read about Atlanta's creeks and forests in the 1980s, the more I learned about the infamous Atlanta child murders. For a nightmarish period between 1979 and 1981, a Black child went missing in Atlanta nearly every month. Twenty-nine cases were linked to one killer, and many of the victims' bodies turned up on riverbanks and vacant wooded lots of Southside Atlanta.[8]

On November 1, 1980, the tiny body of Aaron Jackson Jr., age nine, was spotted by a passerby from the South River Bridge, one block north of Lake Charlotte Nature Preserve. I was shocked to come across a photo of the crime scene on an amateur true crime website that revealed brown ankles in black sneakers laid out on stone riprap. "I wish I hadn't seen the body," Jackson's father told the newspaper after identifying the child at the city morgue. "That's what I see every time I close my eyes."[9]

The ongoing horror of those killings profoundly affected Atlantans' perception of urban waterways and wilderness for years. The murders deepened Whites' fears about the dangers of the inner city, accelerating White flight into the suburbs. And an entire generation of Black

residents learned to fear and avoid Atlanta's forests and rivers. In 1981, Lake Charlotte made headlines when a body was found in the lake. A twenty-seven-year-old lawyer named William Brown was beaten and dumped by muggers from the Cabbagetown neighborhood. Officially, the city breached Lake Charlotte's earthen dam and drained the lake in 1982 in compliance with the US Safe Dams Act. Unofficially, it was haunted.[10]

Lischkoff combined the Lake Charlotte parcel with 163 more acres, citing vague plans to create an industrial park. After a long and losing battle to get the parcel rezoned, it was he, not the city, who sold what was once a public nature preserve to Waste Management.[11]

**I FINALLY EXPLORED** Lake Charlotte Nature Preserve in April 2019 when my colleague Ryan Gravel, an urban planner, got a key to the padlock. He was working on a project for the city, a very Mastroianni kind of plan to preserve the remaining forests of Atlanta. Using the heat map from Trees Atlanta and penalty funds paid by developers who cut down trees, the city was looking to buy forested land and make it publicly accessible. Forty years after the first attempt, this nature preserve seemed like a viable project again.[12]

I drove to Lake Charlotte one warm afternoon with all these stories in my head, bubbling over with Internet research and rumors about a place I had never actually seen. Stacy Funderburke, an attorney with the Conservation Fund who had been working on behalf of the city to buy the property from Waste Management, met Ryan and me on the corner of Forrest Circle. This was one of the Black neighborhoods that fought the landfill and won. I parked in front of a modest, brick split-level and felt conspicuously White piling into Stacy's Subaru. Would these residents benefit from a nature preserve across the street? Or would it mean a different kind of unwelcome traffic?

We pulled into the gate near the South River Bridge and startled a trio of deer crossing Forrest Park Road. Once inside, we stepped over giant truck tires and a scrum of fresh litter. Hunters snuck in, Stacy told us. They cut the lock off a few times a year and the tire dumpers followed.

With the gate locked behind us, we walked into the trees, following the rutted remains of "Woodsey Way," once a residential street leading to Lake Charlotte's lakefront estates. Up ahead, a pile of tires blackened the forest floor, as if children made a game of rolling downhill tucked inside them. The sounds of the outside world blurred with each step. Beech leaves cast corrugated shadows, blocking out the sky. Stacy pointed out a shagbark hickory, a tree that appears as the shaggy Gandalf of the forest. My contribution was the name of this ghost road, last paved in the 1960s.

Eyeing the diameter of the beech trunks, Stacy guessed some of them were 175 years old. He took photos of Ryan and me gazing up, dwarfed by poplars as we ventured down the trail. At a moss-covered Dead End sign, we continued south on Lake Drive. Ryan and I peeked inside the ruins of a two-story brick lodge. No sign of squatters in the rain-collapsed rooms. We speculated about who lived here and when. By the front porch, I toed a leather roller skate, also covered in moss. Based on the pop-tops on the beer cans and typeface for Diet Pepsi, the litter here was late-'80s vintage. Postapocalyptic scenes like these are why *The Walking Dead* is filmed in Atlanta. Humid overgrowth devours a house in no time.

Further down the road, Stacy spotted a great horned owl moving from tree to tree and quietly screwed a telephoto lens onto his camera. I wandered over to the stone gate of a once grand lake house, testing the ground for hidden wells. Right there among the ruins, I pulled up a historic topographical map on my phone. Structures dotted the road here in 1928, overlooking "Mount Manor Lake."[13]

Later, I would spend countless hours sifting through newspaper archives and old maps, trying to learn who developed Mount Manor Lake in the 1920s. Dr. R. F. Ingram came up several times. He was a prominent Atlanta dentist, businessman, politician, "convicted bootlegger," and president of the Mount Manor Estates Fishing Club. At some point, Woodsey Way became Ingram Drive.[14]

Eventually, reading obituaries and society pages, I found a Charlotte in the Ingram family. Miss Charlotte Sage, a wealthy, well-documented Ansley Park debutante of the 1937 season, was Dr. R. F. Ingram's only granddaughter. For years, her outfits and social "gaieties" were

breathlessly chronicled in the Atlanta society pages. Even after Miss Charlotte's wedding to a naval officer in 1948, the papers continued to cover the celebrity couple.[15]

The notice of Charlotte's funeral in 1956 surprised me. She was only thirty-seven years old, without a husband or heirs. It said nothing about how she died, and my imagination filled the blank space with a tragic scandal. Her named vanished from the newspapers, but by 1960, Lake Charlotte appeared on Atlanta maps, a watery tribute that outlasted the lake itself.[16]

As a girl, did Charlotte love this place? I wondered about this as I balanced on a log to cross the creek. I could hear Ryan's and Stacy's voices moving up the hill towards the landfill. My T-shirt clung to my back as I hiked up the shady hillside, past holly bushes and boulders scarred with mossy divots. Thousands of years before Muscogee-speaking people settled here, between 1500 and 600 BCE, people sat on this hillside carving bowls out of the dark green stone. Geologists called it Soapstone Ridge, and archaeologists in the late 1970s made a heroic effort to document the ancient quarry sites and recover priceless stone artifacts before they vanished under landfills and truck lots.[17]

At the top of the hill, the sound of whirring machinery broke the spell. Ryan and Stacy were taking photos of the landfill's blank backside, a grassy expanse pocked with shiny, expensive-looking machinery. No doubt, a surveillance camera somewhere was watching us. I held my breath until I was hidden by the trees again. I spotted at least three strange devices before I googled the name for them—piezometer, an instrument that measures the pressure of groundwater. It reminded me that the Waste Management's greenspace served a purpose, filtering and buffering contaminants from Live Oak. We joked, uneasily, about the chemical odor of the landfill, and what might be in the water.

The afternoon shadows grew long, but we refused to leave until we reached the lake, or what was left of it. We tromped down the hill toward the creek bed. The sky opened up in the clearing where the lake used to be. The plush, sun-dappled floodplain was dotted with lowland sycamores, patches of cattails shifted in the breeze. The shadows of turkey vultures and hawks crossed the swaying lake bottom like fish used to do.

What we found was probably more like what was here before the Ingram family. It was what the Muscogee-speaking people might have seen, and the clans before them—a clearing with a thin creek snaking through it. With the landfill now closed, there was a good chance the park's time had come. What would it mean for the residents in the shadow of those landfills, with gentrification closing in?

When I got home later that night, still high from forest bathing, grainy ringlets plastered to my neck and perfumed with Deet, I found my husband reading in a corner armchair, the kids already in bed. I practically twirled in the door, wanting to tell him about this mysterious place. I tried to pull him away from his reading, suggesting that he come upstairs and check me for ticks. The forest can do that to you—remind you of your animal flesh, your short lifespan—even in the middle of Atlanta.

Within a couple years, Black Atlantans who were promised a park in the '70s and fought the landfill in the '90s will finally be able to walk past the chainlink fence, owners of a place that was off limits for generations. Their grandchildren's inheritance is not just the land, but the chance to "lose themselves" in a carefully managed wilderness in a way that their parents never could. Soon, too, White families like mine that have never ventured to this corner of Atlanta will discover those woods on afternoon picnics, marveling at the beech trees and soapstone boulders.

Enshrined as a nature preserve, what will we name the place? Should we erase Charlotte Sage, ill-fated princess of Mount Manor Lake? Or honor Ted Mastroianni, Aaron Jackson Jr., or Herman Lischkoff—all of the figures whose fates entwined with the place and made it so difficult to bulldoze? Whatever we call it, I hope it will honor the countless Southside neighbors who organized to prevent Lake Charlotte from becoming a dumping ground. This is their victory and their park. ⑤

1   Fulton County GIS, Property Map Viewer, accessed April 13, 2021, https://gis.fultoncountyga. gov/Apps/PropertyMapViewer/; DeKalb County Parcel Viewer, accessed April 13, 2021, https:// dekalbgis.maps.arcgis.com/apps/webappviewer/index.html?id=f241af753f414cdfa31c1fdef0924584.

2   Eric Stirgus, "Landfill Foes Plan Monday Rally at Capitol," *Atlanta Journal-Constitution*, April 4, 2002; Kimberly H. Byrd, "'Enough Is Enough,' Landfill Foes Say," *Atlanta Constitution*, January 28, 1999; David Pendered, "Battle Brewing over Landfill Proposal," *Atlanta Constitution*, August 30, 1994.

3   Hal Lamar, "Residents Rally against Live Oak Extension," *Atlanta Voice*, November 15, 2003; Eric Stirgus, "Officials: Shut Landfill in '04," *Atlanta Journal-Constitution*, May 13, 2003.

4   "Metro Scenes: DeKalb. Indian Relics," *Atlanta Constitution*, May 9, 1984; Stirgus, "Officials"; "Atlanta's Live Oak Landfill to Become Source of Renewable Energy," Renewable Energy World, September 21, 2007.

5   Atlanta Bureau of Parks and Recreation, *The 1975 Annual Report*, Planning Atlanta Planning Publications Collection, Georgia State University Library, p. 1, https://digitalcollections.library.gsu. edu/digital/collection/planATLpubs/id/24207/rec/1.

6   Barry King, "Atlanta Decides to Construct Own Campsites," *Atlanta Constitution*, June 8, 1979; Jay Lawrence, "Atlanta Putting Emphasis on Open Space for Parks," *Atlanta Constitution*, March 17, 1977.

7   Atlanta Regional Commission, *Areawide Outdoor Recreation Planning in the Atlanta Region: Proposed Nature Preserves*, 1979, Planning Atlanta Planning Publications Collection, Georgia State University Library, https://digitalcollections.library.gsu.edu/digital/collection/planATLpubs/id/751/rec/2.

8   Nehl Horton, "City Accepts Bid on Lake Charlotte Land, but Loses $145,756 with the Decision," *Atlanta Constitution*, May 1, 1986.

9   Brenda Mooney, "Slain Youngster Had Been Told to Be Careful," *Atlanta Constitution*, November 4, 1980.

10  Tony Cooper, "Lawyer's Body Found in S.E. Atlanta Lake," *Atlanta Constitution*, September 29, 1981; Charles Anderson, "Neighborhoods: NPU-T Oks Redevelopment Plan, Conditionally," *Atlanta Constitution*, March 18, 1982.

11  Nehl Horton, "Beverly Hills Residents Applaud Zoning Denial," *Atlanta Constitution*, February 20, 1986.

12  "Tree Canopy Atlanta," Center for GIS at Georgia Tech, Trees Atlanta, 2015, http://geospatial. gatech.edu/TreesAtlanta/.

13  "Atlanta 1927–30 Topographic Maps with Open Street Map Overlay," Emory Center for Digital Scholarship, accessed April 13, 2021, http://disc.library.emory.edu/atlanta1928topo/.

14  "Dr. R. F. Ingram, Candidate for Council from Second Ward," *Atlanta Georgian and News*, September 21, 1908, Digital Library of Georgia, https://gahistoricnewspapers.galileo.usg.edu/lccn/ sn89053728/1908-09-21/ed-1/seq-14/print/image_632x817_from_2144,81_to_4260,2813/.

15  "Miss Charlotte Sage to Make Debut at Reception on Dec. 22," *Atlanta Constitution*, September 27, 1936.

16  "Mrs. Charlotte S. McKnight Dies; Funeral to be Today," *Atlanta Constitution*, March 14, 1956.

17  DeKalb County Planning Department, *Soapstone Ridge: Its Environment and Land Use*, June 1976, Planning Atlanta, Planning Publications Collection, Georgia State University Library, https:// digitalcollections.library.gsu.edu/digital/collection/planATLpubs/id/34120/rec/23.

poetry by **Jessica Jacobs**

# Make a fence

said the rabbis, *around the Torah*. And this world
is lousy with them. More than we can count
on our dog walk alone: chainlink and stone and white

wooden pickets. Fences to keep people's bad barking dogs
in, to keep our bad barking dog out. His nostrils flaring
wide as a twirled skirt as he reads the tales of past passersby

on fences that mark what is another's burden, another's
privilege to tend, and what is open to the traffic of strangers.
Called before the Torah, a reader tracks the cramped letters

with a yad, a metal pointer topped by a tiny pointing hand.
If it feels colder than the air, it's because silver steals
your body's heat, this tool to keep your place, to keep you

in your place, to keep you from marring even a single sacred letter.
This, one fence among many: Do not bring the Torah
in the bathroom, do not sit beside it on a bench, do not stand before it

naked (lest you be buried naked, stripped of all the good you did).
But sometimes barriers grow so large it's hard to see
what they're protecting. And here is the fig tree yearning

past its yard, reaching toward the walk with its fat-fingered leaves.
Here, the arbor propping branches slumped as the shoulders
of a weary giant—yet under its hunch, an exuberance of mulberries.

There, the yellow house whose bramble is more than worth its thorns:
drops of ink dripping from the branches, the blackberries call us
to make a quill of our tongues. Let every fence in my mind have a gate.

One with an easy latch and well-oiled hinges. Our neighbors
urge us to indulge—*There's more than we can possibly eat*—so
here, love, is fruit with the sun still inside it. Let me

thumb the juice from your chin. Let us honor what we love
                                by taking it in.

# Contributors

**CICI CHENG** is a Chinese-born US photographer who grew up in Durham, North Carolina. Her work focuses on family, identity, and cultural transition through visual storytelling. A passionate educator, she continues to explore and teach about finding the edges of self-comfort. Cheng is currently teaching at Duke Kunshan University.

**DENIZ DASER** is an anthropologist who studies migration, labor, and citizenship. She is an external lecturer at University of St. Gallen and holds a PhD in anthropology from Rutgers University. Her dissertation, "Leveraging Labor in New Orleans: Worklife and Insecurity among Honduran Migrants," drew upon extensive fieldwork in New Orleans.

**BURAK ERDIM** is associate professor of architectural history and design at North Carolina State University. His research traces the operations of transnational planning cultures and his recent book, *Landed Internationals: Planning Cultures, the Academy, and the Making of the Modern Middle East*, was published by the University of Texas Press (2020).

**SARAH FOUTS** is assistant professor in the Department of American Studies at the University of Maryland, Baltimore County, and holds a PhD in Latin American studies from Tulane University. Fouts is currently working on a book manuscript on labor, migration, food, and transnationalism in post-Katrina New Orleans and Honduras.

**STEVE GALLO** is a historian and writer who recently completed his PhD in the Department of American and Canadian Studies at the University of Nottingham (UK). His work focuses on the use of public parks as a means of economic stimulation and social control in service of the New South movement.

**JOHN LUSK HATHAWAY** was born in Memphis, Tennessee. He received his MFA from East Tennessee State University in 2012. Nominated for the Baum Award, he received the Individual Artist Fellowship Grant from the Tennessee Arts Commission in 2014. Hathaway is an adjunct professor of photography at the College of Charleston.

**ENDIA L. HAYES** is a doctoral student in sociology at Rutgers University, New Brunswick. Her work engages methods of alternative archiving among Afro-Texans by tracing sensorial, sonic, affective, and immaterial embodiments as a map of early twentieth-century Texas. She is also a contributor to Environmental History Now (EHN).

**ALEX HOFMANN** is a PhD candidate in history at the University of Chicago, completing his dissertation, "Southern Sublime: Legacies of Civil War Violence in the New South." In the fall, he will be a teaching fellow in the Division of the Social Sciences and the College at the University of Chicago.

**JESSICA JACOBS** is the author of *Take Me with You, Wherever You're Going*, winner of the Devil's Kitchen and Goldie Awards, and *Pelvis with Distance*, winner of the New Mexico Book Award. Chapbook editor for *Beloit Poetry Journal*, she coauthored *Write It! 100 Poetry Prompts to Inspire* with her wife, Nickole Brown.

Political geographer **MARK LONG** is professor of political science at the College of Charleston, and curator-at-large and academic liaison at its Halsey Institute of Contemporary Art. His research is concerned with intersections between visual culture and place in settings as varied as Antarctica, Israel, and the American South.

**HENRY KNIGHT LOZANO** is senior lecturer in American history and liberal arts at the University of Exeter. He is the author of *Tropic of Hopes: California, Florida, and the Selling of American Paradise, 1869–1929* (2013) and *California and Hawai'i Bound: US Settler Colonialism and the Pacific West, 1848–1959* (2021), and coeditor of *The Shadow of Selma* (2018).

**HANNAH S. PALMER** is author of the award-winning memoir *Flight Path: A Search for Roots Beneath the World's Busiest Airport*. A native of Atlanta's Southside, her writing about place is informed by her work as urban designer. Since 2017, she has led a campaign to restore the urban headwaters of Georgia's Flint River.

**CLAIRE RAYMOND** is the author of eight books of critical theory examining feminism and race, including *The Photographic Uncanny: Photography, Homelessness, and Homesickness* (Palgrave, 2019) and *The Selfie, Temporality, and Contemporary Photography* (Routledge, 2021). She was a faculty member at the University of Virginia for many years and is now a visiting research collaborator at Princeton University.

**ANNIE SIMPSON**, a multi-/inter-/un- disciplined artist, was born in North Carolina and is currently an MFA candidate at the University of Georgia. She was a 2019 Monument Lab Fellow (as part of Take Action Chapel Hill) and has forthcoming exhibitions with the Goethe-Institut North America. She has exhibited recently at the Carrack (Durham), Purdue University, the University of Georgia, and the University of North Carolina.

**JACQUELINE TAYLOR** is an architectural and art historian working at the intersection of race, gender, and the urban environment. She received her MA and PhD from the University of Virginia, where she also studied historic preservation. She has taught and published widely on modernism and the Black experience.

# Order now or give a gift . . .